CRACKINGTON HAVEN

A CENTURY OF CHANGE
THE MEMOIRS OF ALFRED THOMAS TILLEY

J

JAISLAMEEGO PUBLISHING

Published by:
Jaislameego Publishing
Tel: 01237 423009

First published 2016

ISBN 978-0-9955090-0-9 paperback

British Library Cataloguing-in-Publication Data
A catalogue record for this book is available from the British Library

FSC® C013056
MIX
Paper from responsible sources
www.fsc.org

Typeset by Streamline Photography & Design, Devon. www.streamlinepad.co.uk
Printed and bound by Biddles, Kings Lynn, Norfolk

Front cover image: Crackington Haven © Julia Woolgar
Back cover image: Portrait of Alfred Thomas Tilley © Julia Woolgar

Contents

Introduction

This is not an academic book, I am just an ordinary man who has had the privilege of enjoying a long life in one of the most beautiful areas along the North Cornwall coast. Over the past century I have collected a scrapbook of notes, memorabilia and some faded photographs, but I am not a historian. I am often asked questions about this and that, so I thought it time to compile a book where I can share some memories of the past. It is a candid account of life as I remember it, though everyone has their own memories and may have seen things from a different perspective. My ancestors have lived in this area for hundreds of years and our extensive families had filled the parish. I was born during the First World War, at a time when everyone lived off the land. Farming and earning a living in this area was a challenge to say the least! I've had a few scrapes and on all accounts I shouldn't be here to tell the tale, but at present I'm still out and about enjoying life.

I've seen a century of changes and some I would never have thought possible. From horses and wagons to the first motor vehicles and petrol station in the haven. Like all people I have been through ups and downs, I survived the war and sought to earn a living in a quiet country area. I am often asked the secret of long life. Experts say there are five things. I'm no authority on the subject but I agree and can expand upon: 1. Good family life; 2. Social activity with friends; 3. Environment and exercise; 4. Home cooked food, (with pasties and porridge); and 5. A positive attitude. My eldest sisters are still alive and I am sure they would agree that it sums up our life. I've been clubbing since my teens, enjoy a good social life and have had a plentiful share of the good life with wholesome food and natural exercise. There are folks who would like to get back to being self sufficient, the way we were. You can never get it back the same. Like so many good things you don't always fully appreciate them until they're gone. There is no dress rehearsal for life, I've learnt that lesson.

Cornwall is like a picture within a beautiful frame. It's first known for the spectacular coastline, being a peninsula you are never far from the sea. It's all enhanced by the mild climate, coastal villages, historic houses and fabulous gardens. I have seen the tourist industry become well established, we worked hard to encourage it and now leisure is the prime activity. This staggering, rugged coastline has attracted many well known celebrities over the years, in more recent times it has become popular with the filming of *Doc Martin*, a series which illustrates the beauty of Cornwall so well that it can be forgiven for the way it depicts the Cornish! We are often viewed as simple, ruthless and uneducated, but the folks I have known have been kindly, intelligent, hard-working and extremely hospitable. Everyone agrees Crackington is a special place. Sometimes beautiful areas become a victim of their own success. I sincerely hope Crackington will remain a haven of tranquillity and peace, a very special place for all the generations to come.

Alfred Thomas Tilley

Crackington Haven in 2016

Courtesy © Streamline Photography & Design

Crackington Manor Estate History

The original thatched Manor House and mill

The Manor has a long history; it was mentioned in the Domesday Book of 1086 when William the Conqueror awarded a total of 797 Manors to Robert. Robert lived in France and his property was administered from Launceston in Cornwall and Montacute in Somerset. The value dropped to ten shillings as Crackington Manor had previously been occupied and valued at £1. A lot of ancient history has been found in and around St Gennys. Iron Age hill forts, Celtic, Medieval and Roman artefacts had been found here. Over the years a number of archaeologists and geologists have visited the area. The Attenborough family visited Crackington and stayed locally. I remember another man who stayed here; I believe he was an archaeologist digging into the history of Tresmorn. He lived in a caravan for some months and used to buy paraffin from us, for cooking and light. One day he came to the garage as a strong south westerly gale had blown his caravan over. He assured us all was well because he managed to fix and arrange everything on the side and could climb in through the top. Then would you believe it, the wind turned around and a strong gust blew the caravan back up again! We were left puzzled as to what happened to the paraffin lamps and stove but he assured us they had righted themselves as well!

In 1911 my grandfather Thomas Tilley was a tenant of Crackington Manor, he paid £65 per year for 106 acres of land at Hill Farm. Thomas was my grandfather, he was a farmer but had served as a policeman in his younger days. My grandparents were ready for retirement by the time my parents were married, so my father ran the farm. My eldest sister Lottie was born at Hill and I came along the following year. My earliest recollections are scanty but I vaguely remember being in a pushchair. My parents used to visit the Marshalls at Tresparret and something must have stuck in my mind as I can recall being wrapped up in a blanket in very blustery weather. My father used to talk about the old cemetery up at Hill Farm, which may have been the site of an old church with an ancient burial ground. No one was sure but they found some arched shaped stones which appeared to be old windows. Hill Farm was also mentioned in the Domesday Book so it would have been very old. It was around this time that Squire Robert Harris decided to sell some of the tenanted farms, homesteads and cottages and this would be the first time the Crackington Manor Estate would be split up. The family had a good relationship with Squire Harris and during his time at Hill Farm my father built two cottages on the land, but I'm not sure how that came about.

Crackington Manor Estate
The first auction
These days you would need to add a few noughts but it was all comparable to income back then.

Red Lion Inn to Mr Marshall for £400
Roundhouse to Mr Sandercock for £3,000
Hill Farm to Mr Tucker for £1,400
Bay Park to Mr Tinney for £1,700
Hallagather to Mr Rogers for £1,700
Hole Farm to Mr Gliddon for £1,000
Bay Park to Mr Ward for £60
Higher Crackington to Mr Spry for £500
Sweets to Mr Sandercock for £210
Landsweden to Mr Coombe for £66
Tresparret to Mr Sandercock for £20
Pengold to Mr Spry for £500
Lower and Middle Crackington to Mr Ward for £4,200

As for Crackington Manor itself, there had been many owners but few had lived there. It was an ancient stone and thatched Manor House with an open courtyard, stable block and a working watermill serving the surrounding tenanted farms.

Crackington Manor House, mill & stable block, the ford across the river to the Miller's Cottage, now Little Pen

Loaded wagons used to come down from the top of the hills through Ludon Valley, it was the easiest and most direct route to the haven. With a millpond and river in close proximity the Manor was damp and liable to flooding. Not as one might imagine a Manor House and estate today. In 1889 Captain Teague sold the Manor to Mr Batchelor who in turn sold it to Squire Harris. The watermill had become obsolete. Robert Harris became Lord of the Manor and turned it into an elaborately modern residence for his own use. In July 1920 Squire Robert Harris sold Crackington Manor and the remainder of the tenanted farms, homesteads, cottages and building sites.

Crackington Manor Estate
The second auction
Stretches along the North Cornish Coast with an unbroken seaboard to the Atlantic

for over two miles from the haven at Crackington to the Boscastle district, and is justly tamed for the grandeur of its rugged cliff scenery and the beauty of its inland valleys and woodlands. The property was divided into eight lots:

Lot 1 – Crackington Manor, an elaborately equipped residence with 21 acres of land
Lot 2 – Trevigue Farm with 492 acres of land
Lot 3 – Tremoutha Ball with 184 acres of land
Lot 4 – Ludon Farm with 50 acres of land
Lot 5 – A rood odd allotment
(old English for a ¼ acre plot)
Lot 6 – Building site with 3 acres
Lot 7 – Building site with 1½ acres
Lot 8 – Building site

The Manor was described as an exceptionally well built modern residence with a lovely situation and facing the Atlantic Ocean. The house contains:

Ground floor: hall, drawing room, 31ft billiard room, 17ft dining room, 3 bedrooms and a water closet
First floor: 4 bedrooms, dressing rooms, bathroom, linen cupboard, WC.
Second floor: 3 bedrooms
Basement: kitchens, pantry, servants hall, store room, larder, dairy etc
Grounds: flower and vegetable gardens, 2 good sized tennis courts, trout stream, good stabling for 5 horses with a large coach house and a harness room
Coachman's cottage with 3 good size bedrooms

My parents purchased the Manor with 21 acres of land which extended from the beach up the valley, predominately on the south side of Crackington. The Parnell family bought Ludon and Tremoutha with over 230 acres of land extending further south in the direction of Boscastle. The Crackington Manor Estate had now been completely divided up and it was the end of an era.

A Fresh Start
At the top of Crackington my grandfather John Ward built Crackington Vean for his

Billiard Room, Manor House

retirement. The site chosen enabled him to have a choice view over the fields and down the valley to the haven. It was an imposing gentleman's residence with servants' quarters. Across the valley on the north side, his friend George Parnell had retired from the aircraft industry in Bristol and he also built an imposing gentleman's residence with servants' quarters, Nancemellon at the top of Pentreath hill. The men were great buddies and arranged to build their homes on opposite sides of the valley so they could send signals to each other – there were no telephones in those days.

Crackington Vean on the right skyline and Uncle Stephen's chicken farm at Trethew

My Uncle Edgar Ward farmed at Crackington Farm and Uncle Frank Ward farmed at Flanders, while Uncle Stephen Ward built a chicken farm at Trethew. All these farms had land on the south side of Crackington. Aunt Loveday married Mark Gliddon and farmed at Hole, whilst Thomas married Gertrude Stephens and they farmed at Pencuke. Then Elizabeth married West Stephens who lived at Home Farm in Boscastle. My Uncle Charlie married Alice and they moved to London. Edward married May and Jane

married Fred Edwards and they built Little Melrose. I think I can safely say we were a farming community! The land at Crackington Manor joined the boundary of Flanders Farm on the southern slopes in the heart of the valley and my grandfather had a bird's-eye view from the top.

I was three years old when we moved into the Manor. My elder sister was five and by then she would have been starting school, the same school as our mother and father had attended many years before. My parents had married prior to the First World War at Brockhill, the chapel on the south side of Crackington. It was a perfect union and they had an enthusiastic start farming at Hill. They could never have guessed the world would be turned upside down within a few years. The Great War came as a shock; it claimed many local young men including my mother's brother. My eldest sister Lottie and I were born during it and I came into the world a few weeks after my uncle Alfred was killed in the Battle of the Somme. It was supposed to be the war to end all wars so my parents were determined to work hard together and create a brighter future. Crackington Manor was a very big house for a young family of four but my parents had ambitious plans to turn it into a self-sufficient guest house and farm. I grew up working alongside my father and boy did he work! From the break of dawn we would feed the animals and milk the cows and then work through until dusk. Additionally my father converted Manor Cottage into a comfortable residence for my grandparents, Thomas and Grace.

My father holding the reigns

The Haven in 1920

That alone was a major undertaking as previously the only habitable part had been upstairs. In those days the ceilings were lath and plaster and the walls were stone. A kitchen was installed downstairs with a very old-fashioned range, which, if I remember correctly, came out of the old Manor House. A large ceramic sink and local slate flag stone floors also proved to be heavy work. It's probably all in vogue again now! Manor Cottage had been the harness and tack rooms with the coachman's quarters above. With my grandparents happily occupying their retirement home my father turned his attention to transforming the Manor into a fully functional hotel by the sea. The stable was in the old courtyard along with another long barn which had seen better days, so the entire courtyard area was rebuilt as an additional wing providing several new bedrooms with a large garage underneath. My father had already built two cottages and, although self taught, he clearly knew what he was doing. I was very young when we worked together, he taught me traditional crafts and skills that I have never forgotten. He was a positive, forward-thinking man with progressive ideas, which I admired.

In the 1920s there were no stores selling building supplies like we see today. It's hard to imagine now but we made everything from the materials we had at hand. The complete opposite to methods employed today where folks work out

1920s building works

footbridge across the river. The ford between the Manor and Little Pen eventually became obsolete. At that time there were only a small number of very old buildings in Crackington itself: The Manor and Manor Cottage, Ludon, Mascott, Coombe Barton, Penkenna House, Little Pen and the Old Thatched Cottages. The number of dwellings in the haven has more than doubled in my lifetime. Most of the sites were cut out of the hills involving massive excavations. The spoils of earth mounds were dumped on our land because in those days there

what they need and then buy it in – back then we looked around at what he had and worked out how to use it! It is so different these days and I wonder what my father would think if he could see one of the super DIY stores or builders merchants. There was a water-powered saw bench where we cut and sliced wood. That alone was heavy and demanding work and was probably a vast improvement on the saw pit, but still required immense strength to provide enough wood for the home-made carpentry throughout. I had a big pad for mixing mortar and there was scaffolding, as the whole building tied in with the existing Manor which was very high. The scaffold poles were later turned into handrails for bridges and for fencing off areas; there may even be a few around today. By the time we had finished I felt like I had served an apprenticeship in all aspects of building. Being so close to the river, the banks had to be built up in order to prevent flooding – there seemed no end to the work! Originally there were two fords in the haven, one where the road bridge is now and the other beside the

William (left), Kate with young Alfred, Lottie and family

wasn't the means of removing it. Old photos show the big heaps of earth and rock on both sides of the haven. Gunnedah and Paramatta were built on top of Mill Ball hill and that completely changed the approach to the haven, it significantly altered the landscape. There was talk of creating a road from Hill through Ludon to the Haven, the route the wagons used to take down to the Mill, this would have overcome problems with the sharp bend at the top of Mill Ball hill, but in the event it was decided against.

Young Alfred

While all this work was going on my mother attended to the domestic duties. Then again she never went to a shop, and how she cared for two youngsters, did all the domestic work and helped with the farm I will never know! She worked fast and often preferred to work alone – she would kill four or five chickens and have them plucked, pulled and presented oven-ready. The kitchens and dairy were well equipped and my mother spent most of her time there, cooking, cleaning, washing and stoking the range and fires. There were fires in nearly all the rooms, most big enough to take large logs which were rolled forward when lit and rolled back if we moved to another room. Pasties would be made and crimped a dozen or more at a time – she was unstoppable! My mother was a quiet, unassuming, modest woman who thoroughly enjoyed being hospitable and was happy providing for others. It took a while to establish the guest house as my parents had so much work to do. Father installed plumbing and attended auctions to furnish the house from top to bottom. My mother made curtains and soft furnishings and clothes – she would embroider, sew and knit. There were some

large windows upstairs; the French doors to the veranda were dressed with plush red velvet and lace. As you would expect in that time period everything was Victorian styling as that was the fashion. I wouldn't describe them as a fashionable couple; far from it! Yet they furnished their home with all the comfort and style expected at that time.

When I look back now at what my parents accomplished, I realise I took so much of it for granted, I thought everyone lived like that. My father was very tall and strong; he set a high standard, which as a boy I found very demanding. He was a man mountain, with big hands that tossed great weights and bales of hay into the air. We often laugh at the wheelbarrow he made, it was solid oak with iron wheels

Kate

which no one else could lift off the ground, let alone load it and push it! Yet for all his strength he was kindly, gregarious, docile and stoic. A typical Cornish farmer with the manners and style of a country gentleman. Now I understand how he trained me and taught us skills for life. There is no doubt in my mind that those early days contributed to my continued good health, stamina and attitude to life. Now I regret that I didn't appreciate my parents more. How they kept busy and positive, accepting challenges and working by initiative. They thoroughly understood the countryside and their natural surroundings. Everything was recycled, sustainable and renewable, something the world is struggling to replicate today. It may have been hard work but it was enjoyable, satisfying, healthy and an exceptionally good life.

Crackington Manor became a successful country hotel where all the food was produced from the farm. In the main season my mother would prepare and cook for up to 50 guests a day, all served in the upstairs dining room, while downstairs in the living room a dining table was always open to our many relations, friends and strangers. It was hospitality on the highest level, generous and with the warmest welcome. I smile these days when I see a hospitality tray with a tiddly teapot, squirt of milk and a few knobs of sugar. I would like to see my mother's face! Guests would have their clothes washed and shoes cleaned. After a decade spent establishing the business my parents produced another three children, by then

my eldest sister and I could help, we left school at fourteen and worked at home.

The summer ended with Bude Fair and this was an annual, well deserved treat for my mother. She really looked forward to meeting up with family and friends and they really enjoyed it. Not the sort of fair you would see today, more like a farmers'

Alfred with young sister (Crossley in background)

market with trade stalls and livestock such as geese. You can imagine the scene as steam tractors powered the swings, roundabouts and the fairground organ. There were portable theatres presenting short performances and it would be very jolly. My mother was a very content person and she loved Crackington to the extent that she never travelled away from Cornwall. My father, on the other hand, used to spend a week in Hendon with my uncle Charlie Ward. London was the home of the Motor Show and an annual treat for the men. When I was younger I viewed my parents as old-fashioned and I suppose that's typical of youngsters. It's only when you get older yourself that you realise each generation has its own lifestyle and, before you know it, you're old-fashioned yourself! As a young couple, my parents took on an ambitious project when the hospitality industry was just beginning. I realise now they were proactive, creative, a genuine honest couple who were interested in the welfare of others and treated everyone with respect and dignity. Qualities that were prevalent years ago, which built strong families and communities. In recent times I've been to all the usual places where you see antiques, vintage and historic stuff. Family take me along but after a good look around I realise it's all very familiar to me and nothing seems old. It can be a shock to see the price of some things we used to cut up for scrap or bury years ago. Things change over time and you don't always realise how fast the years fly by. In fact the truth is, it is we ourselves that fly by and before you know it we are looking back over time.

William Thomas

Little Pen (miller's cottage) & The Old Thatched Cottages

The Manor House

Farm, Dairy and Kitchen

Making hay in the tennis court

From my earliest years I worked alongside my father on the farm, having left school at 14-years-old. Winters were much harder then with snow, frost, solid ice, freezing conditions and frozen ground. Surrounded as we were by steep hills it was not unusual to be cut off from civilisation. Animals to be fed and the high stacks of summer hay dwindling, it seemed like we always had a good six months of hard winter hoping that spring would not be late. Once thawed the ground would turn to mud half way up our boots! You could guarantee that on wet, windy days the cows would take themselves up to the highest point of the green fields by Flanders. Boots squelched and sucked through a muddy track to the top of the hill to fetch them in. We had a dog but he found it a chore and nearly always decided to lay down for a rest halfway! If I called the cows they would ignore me, playing deaf so they could munch another tuft of grass. Then, as I got nearer the field, they would look up at me with udders full to leaking point. We waddled down the track, their hooves and hind legs sinking ever deeper into the sticky mud. Cows are very inquisitive creatures and stop to look around before making it down into the cowshed, where it was a time consuming job of washing and milking each one by hand. Feeding, mucking out and swilling down leaving it clean for the next session. Calves were kept in the cowshed, they were fed scalded milk from a bucket and united with their mums after milking, that way

Farming in the Haven

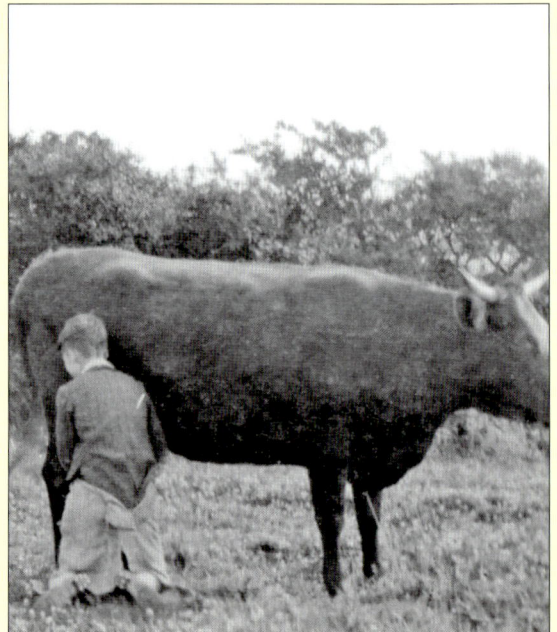

the calves weren't hungry and could just enjoy mum's company. Most people in the parish kept a cow, pig and a few chickens in an outhouse, it seemed the natural thing to do. We kept about four milking cows. Like us the animals love the spring, they frisk and skip about. It is one of the joys of the countryside to see them out in the fields, all part of the rich cycle of life. These days farming has become a factory, with mechanical production driven by price. It's all on a larger scale now with vast sheds filled with hundreds of cows, kept inside year round under artificial light. Everything is geared to producing tank loads of milk. Some cows never see the open fields, tread green grass or get the sun on their backs! I never liked the idea of battery hens either, those birds never saw an egg! Everything was more natural when I was young, no one ever told us how many buckets of milk we could produce and we certainly never threw any away.

Market days were a feature and all animals were walked there. There were no lorries then and this was a task I dreaded. I had to take the cow to the bull at Crackington Farm, which belonged to my uncle Edgar Ward. After walking the cow about a mile up the road, we entered the yard and my uncle would let the bull loose. I was terrified! These were massive animals with immense strength. I never trusted them and I was really scared! These days with larger herds, farms keep their own bull or call on the services of artificial insemination. This is one thing I would probably have welcomed wholeheartedly as by then I had

developed a morbid fear of bulls! I have lived long enough to see a century of farming. In my early years I found it very hard and physically demanding. I always had a shovel in my hand. My father used to cut hay by hand using a scythe, he took the lead and set the pace for us to follow and there would be an entire meadow to cut in a day. Following that the horses were used to turn the hay and collect onto

My mother Kate

the wagon. A large hayrick was built near the cowshed ready for the winter. Tractors didn't arrive on the scene until the 1930s and even then my father never had one. It is a marked contrast from the early days until now. On the downside it seems only the larger farms can survive and they are struggling with diseases and changing weather patterns. On the upside farming has become an industry revolutionised by computerised machinery and labour saving devices that we could never have imagined. The English countryside is unique with its patchwork of green pastures and hedges. These days a dairy farmer goes out of business every day, so it's a good thing that through the ups and downs some have kept up the farming tradition. The landscape wouldn't look the same without it.

We kept a good size poultry house, a shed approximately 30x10 ft. All free range and the hens produced a lot of eggs. There used to be a packing station in Bude and each week they collected the eggs, which we had cleaned and sorted. I was interested in poultry and fascinated by egg production. But killing the birds to eat? There is no easy way to slaughter any livestock, that was another job I felt uncomfortable with. Old friends looking you straight in the eye! The most humane way of killing a chicken requires courage and then to hang them up by the feet to drain. Not an enjoyable job! Plucking and gutting was for the kitchen in those days, all part of the domestic task. Once pulled and cleaned the offal was fed to the eels. The eels were part of the ecosystem, they lived in the river under the footbridge where there were usually about 40 to 50 of them living in a deep pool. They thrived on waste and kept the water quality pure. You rarely see an eel in rivers these days, maybe the odd one or two. Waste has become a huge issue on a larger scale but on a smaller domestic scale it all worked out all right. Cleaning the cows and poultry houses gave us an abundant supply of manure, which was used to replenish the ground. Recycling was a natural process in those days, everything was useful. Big and bulky items in need of disposal would be useful in building

Glasshouses in the asparagus garden

stronger hedges as they could be buried in, stone faced and grassed over. There were no rubbish collections or recycling points and old vehicles or farm implements eventually rusted away and needed disposing of. Eventually everything goes back to the ground. To make the hedges stock proof we used to lay them, that is by partly cutting the tree near the bottom trunk with a bill hook and laying them down in the same direction as the south westerly gales. The bushes would sprout again making the hedge thicker, at the same time soil from the ditches would be cleared and cast up onto the hedge giving fallen seeds a chance to grow. Every ditch in the parish used to be cleared regularly, all cleaned and dug out by hand allowing free flow of surplus water and floods. Hedges were cut back and there was a profusion of birds and wildlife, much more than we see today.

My father would buy in some piglets from Wainhouse Corner market in the early summer. They were kept in the meadow and fed mainly on swill during the summer months. There was always a pig for the salt tub. Pigs were a very important part of the diet and it was usual to fatten pigs for the table. After hanging in the outhouse they would be prepared ready for the tub. Sprinkling table salt for some seasoning is an underestimation of its true value, it was the essential ingredient in preserving food. Salt is able to penetrate both plant and animal cells and will draw water and moisture out which prevents the food from rotting and spoiling. Today meat is processed in a mechanical way, the whole procedure is speeded up and often artificial ingredients added. Freezers and fridges were unheard of when I was young but my parents knew how to preserve a pig! It took time but the flavours were improved and the process produced high quality meat. Also we knew where it came from, what it had been fed and that it had a decent life before the tub. Nothing was wasted, my mother used to stuff the trotters and I loved the fat off the bacon from the ceiling rack. It was delicious, but these days it doesn't taste the same and I no longer enjoy it.

Buckets of milk were delivered to the dairy kitchen twice daily, a constant flow. Large shallow bowls were filled and left to stand, a stove was set aside for making cream, very slowly heating until it formed a crust on the top. After overnight cooling on the slate shelves it was skimmed off the top into cream bowls. The remaining milk was known as scalded milk. There was always a plentiful supply of cream, my mother used it in cooking and we always had a large bowl on the table to add to fruit and vegetables alike. Surplus cream was made into butter. My mother would spend her evenings sat beside the fire always creating something, either sewing, knitting or making butter. It was yellow and I cannot find anything like it today. There is nothing quite like fresh bread with home-made butter. The cool dairy room had a gauze window and large slate shelves laden with bowls of cream, butter and usually a junket. The milk was very rich and creamy, the cows produced several gallons of top-quality milk each day. Nowadays it is accepted that most of it comes from Friesian herds which produce many more gallons, but the quality is not as rich. I for one was addicted to the wonderful taste and, in spite of all the warnings about fat, cream and butter, I have lived long enough to tell the tale!

Cornwall was known for pasties and cream. Visitors revisited year after year to indulge and they liked to take cream home for their friends or even post it! We used to send it from the post office in Crackington. Having come from the cities many of our visitors were keen to help on the farm at harvest time and share the picnic from the harvest hamper. It was always filled with home cooked goodies, pasties, cakes, biscuits and all swilled down with cider or cold tea. Another source of food came from the beach. Living so close to the sea we gathered shellfish and picked winkles, then boiled them in a pot and pickled them in vinegar. Some folks liked limpets! And there was always a plentiful supply of mackerel, cod, bass and other tasty fish along the coast.

Much to my mother's delight, the original cloam oven was uncovered when my father was demolishing a wall in the original Manor house to create the post office sorting room. Father established the first post office in the Haven while mother was well acquainted with cloam ovens and put it into good use. They were made of clay, and there were potteries that produced them in the West Country until the early 1900s. Built into the wall of the fireplace they had a sealed door, which maintained the heat and locked in the flavour. My mother used to light it with faggots of twigs and wood, of which we had a plentiful supply. Often furze (gorse) was used since it lights and burns very easily and is readily available. Once the oven is red hot then the ashes are raked out and the cooking is put in place. The secret is to have everything well prepared in advance. The larger items such as bread, joints and pasties are the first in while the temperature is at its highest, then the smaller items followed. This is cooking on a higher level and the flavour is something I have never forgotten. In my opinion a stove to replicate the cooking of a cloam oven has yet to be invented.

There was a large pine farmhouse table in the downstairs living room of the Manor. It was an open house with tradesman, postman and family all stopping for refreshment. The table would be filled with delicious home cooked fare. My mother had a big black range cooker in the sizeable lower kitchen where she stoked the fire. There was an island with a cool marble top for rolling pastry and another large pine table with drawers for the cooking utensils, plus vast dressers stacked with crockery and jugs. There were a couple of sinks, one with a pump from the well. The draining boards were of heavily scrubbed wood with plate racks above. There was a dumb waiter that hoisted the hot food speedily to the upstairs dining area. Stairs led up to this serving kitchen. Visitors gathered in the dining room, which was light and spacious with a glass roof and a picture window. My sisters Lottie, Eileen and Monica assisted with housekeeping and kitchen duties. Monica was the post office assistant and Roy was the postman amongst other things (my mother, brothers and sisters chose to use their second names). Everyone worked flat out and, even then, we needed to employ extra help in the season. Upstairs there were servants' quarters that we occupied during the summer months. It was a common practice for family members to move out of the main bedrooms in the summer, as every available room would be required for guests. During the winter months, with everyone occupying the main bedrooms, the upstairs kitchen and

spare rooms were used as store rooms with wooden trays of apples and other fruits to see us through the winter.

My mother had been following the same cooking methods for generations. Traditionally mothers taught their daughters to cook and fathers taught their sons gardening and husbandry skills. There were no written recipes and the very old ranges had no temperature gauge; it was a craft that was learnt by experience and taught from an early age.

My mother was often asked for recipes, but she had none. She would explain how she created the different textures and how the mixture should feel by hand – no mixers then! The Cornish pasty has been through some controversy in recent times but in my opinion there is none to be compared to my mother's traditional pasties. The essential ingredient being a good dollop of Cornish cream, which melts between layers of thinly sliced potatoes and onions, some tender chunks of steak all well seasoned with salt and pepper. No one in our family would even begin to make a pasty without a good supply of cream! There were variations of course – potatoes, swede, onion all thinly sliced with plenty of seasoning and cream. For high tea there was always a saffron cake, scones or splits, freshly baked with home-made jam and a good serving of cream on the top! The Cornish have always made wonderful cream teas and years ago many homes opened their gardens to serve the unbeatable combination of jam and cream heaped onto freshly baked scones or splits. It is known as a cream tea and cream is the main ingredient. We always spooned plenty of cream on the top and let the jam soak into the scones. Some folks prefer jam teas with jam on top and that's fine if you need to hide the cream, or haven't got much to spare! At the Manor local families would come and help themselves to the dairy produce, dip their own milk into a small churn, leaving a coin on the shelf. Scalded milk was used for cooking or fed back to the calves, nothing was wasted. We usually had a junket, one of my

favourite desserts made with fresh warm milk straight from the cow, mixed with a spoonful of rennet and sugar, sprinkled with nutmeg, served with a crushed cracker and the essential dollop of cream! It is difficult to buy rennet these days so my favourite pudding, like a lot of things has become a delicacy.

Orchards

Before the war there were many orchards throughout the valley. Below Trethew and throughout the Congdons Valley there were a profusion of fruit trees. The valley used to be divided up with hedges providing protection from the sea winds.

In my youth it was full of blossom in springtime and full of fruit in the autumn. You can imagine how that contributed to the wildlife, birds and bees. It was during the war years that the many orchards were destroyed and the ground ploughed up to become part of the Dig for Victory campaign. During that era the government dictated what and how things should be grown and acres of trees were cut down.

The orchards were my father's pride and joy, there were five altogether and he was meticulous with pruning and caring for the trees. All the fruit trees were the old varieties and, believe me, they tasted good! There were cherries, pears, plums and many different apple trees, including the cider apples. The orchard was located to the east, up in the valley where there was shelter from the south-westerly gales. My father planted copious amounts of daffodils and these were always the first crops in the spring. We gathered them into bunches and delivered them to the Manor where they were packed into boxes. The large kitchen table would be covered with the flowers all bunched and bound by rubber bands. It was a job supervised by my sister Lottie and an ideal task for the children with their nimble fingers. Other boxes would be packed with primroses and violets. I would take the harvest to Otterham Station where they were bound for Covent Garden Market. The spring usually comes early in Cornwall and I seem to remember they made about sixpence a bunch if they were picked and sent early enough. The orchards on the south side of the stream escaped the war but these days there is only one of the original fruit trees surviving. The daffodils, primroses and bluebells faithfully flower year after year and new trees have been planted.

As you would expect my father kept bees in the orchard and managing them was another job I fought shy of! My father had been offered a hive and I went along with him to collect it. Bees do not like being disturbed, but they were all safe inside and we put a sack over the top, secured it and off we went carrying the hive in our hands. Striding out in front, my father was not aware that a few bees were escaping through a small hole in the sack

and already climbing up my arms! Trying to keep calm and be brave I kept going, by the time I raised the alarm the bees had massed together up my sleeves and were swarming towards my chest! At this point, to the disgust of my father, I dropped the hive and started to strip off my clothes. There is a knack to beekeeping, from siting the hive through to collecting the combs dripping with golden honey. Father had everything under control, the sack sorted and the bees delivered safely to their new home in the orchard and from then on I kept clear of them!

Fruit picking was another major task; early crops were picked ready for the table or for sale while the majority of the apples ripened later for storing. Another family effort, climbing wooden ladders and filling baskets to the brim. My mother would provide hampers of pasties and cakes for crib as we called it. In the Manor the fruit was then sorted into wooden boxes to store in the spare rooms upstairs, while downstairs in the kitchen surplus fruit was boiled into chutney, pickles and so forth to fill the pantry. Most of the trees were producing the old traditional varieties of fruit which thrived in this part of the world. Not all varieties grow here; like any plant its location, soil and climate governs success. There was a footbridge over the river to the strawberry field, in front of what is now the Nook. Row upon row of strawberries basked in the sun ready for picking and that was another seasonal task. The slopes on the north side of Crackington made good strawberry beds, gardens facing south are well drained and soak up the sun. The climax of the harvest was the cider making. An annual event, my father would be ready with his cider press. After making a cheese with apples and straw it was then put through the press and stored in old rum casks. The press would be kept busy as locals gathered with their harvested apples with receptacles ready and father would make them some really good Cornish Scrumpy. In the orchard there were trees grown specifically

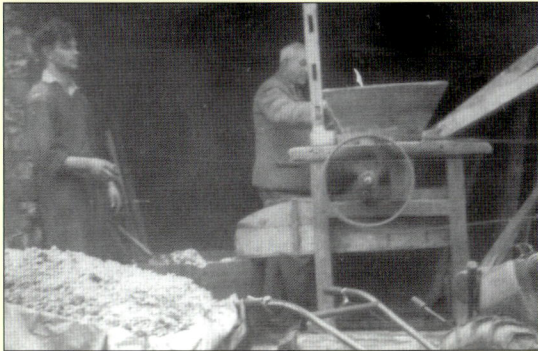

Cider making

for cider making – a cultivar which produces a quality cider. I was never quite sure how it worked as my mother was quietly a very religious woman and never drank alcohol. Cider seemed to be classed in a different category; I suppose it was just viewed as apple juice!

There was a sizeable kitchen garden and glasshouse situated in a sheltered spot beyond the cowshed. This alone took some maintaining as there were currant bushes, gooseberries, raspberries, rhubarb and, amongst other things, a vine in the glasshouse which produced large clusters of dessert grapes. All the vegetables were home-grown and, in addition to this, my father grew a variety of potatoes at Flanders. That was the way it worked years ago, everyone shared labour and produce. My uncle would leave some land for my father to plant and then, come harvest time, he would help gather in my uncle's potatoes as well as his own. There were a lot of exchanges, it was the tradition in the parish and it worked really well. It saved money changing hands and everyone united in their efforts. I remember spending days working up at Tremoutha with Tom and Harry. They used a pole system to gather hay, before that I had been given the job of turning it all! Tom and Harry then came with their horses to help us turn and gather our own harvest. My mother always provided the hampers and lunches; she used a soft, quick cooking variety of potato to make pasties, while other varieties were better suited to roasting. Looking back I would say the flavours were stronger and more distinct and I remember how good things tasted then. Home produced food was excellent quality and had to be a major contributor to good health. I am a decent age with very little sight but I can still cook and bake my own cakes, grow a few beans and tomatoes. I don't like the thought of artificial ingredients and additives that are put into food these days.

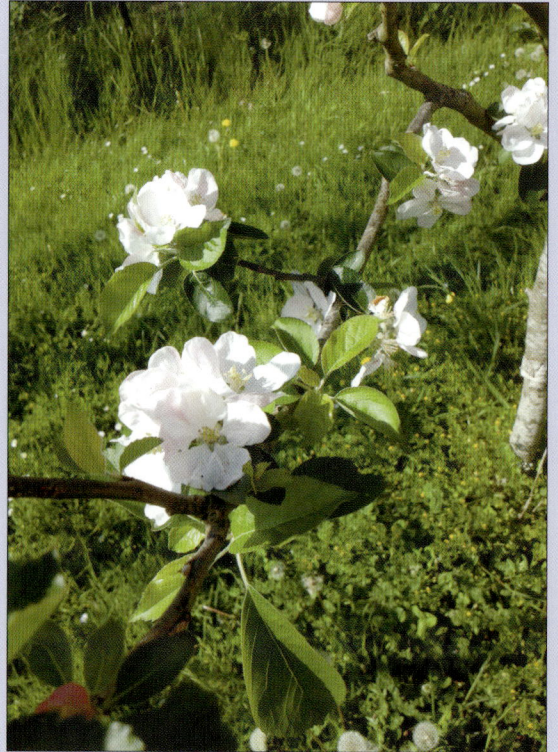

The old orchard a century later – one of the few surviving apple trees

The Millpond

The Miller's Cottage

There was a millpond situated to the east of the Manor's front garden. The mill originally served the surrounding farmers who brought their grain to be ground. Farmers combined their efforts when it came to the harvest, horses were used to pull the wagons and the sheaves were pitched on to the carts. From the south side of Crackington the wagonloads were transported down to the mill through Ludon. The Ludon Valley was a more accessible route to the haven and my father thought that the road would have been built from Hill through to the haven. It was more direct and used to be the easiest way down. The Miller lived at the Miller's Cottage, now Little Pen on the north side of the haven, there used to be a well-used cart track across the ford between Little Pen and the mill at the Manor. The mill was ancient and was demolished long before my father bought the Manor, however the millpond remained up until the late 1960s. The footbridge between north and south is still in existence but the ford and cart track have long since disappeared. Over the years sections of the hillside were cut out and excavated for building, resulting in tons of earth and rock spoil filling the area, riverbanks were built up where the ford crossed the river at the bottom. The footpath between Little Pen and the Manor used to be one of the most popular and well maintained paths in the haven, but it is not so today. The only evidence of the mill these days are the millstones, one became a garden feature at Miller's Cottage, another can be seen at the beach head. The millstone was built into the pillar of the stone bridge; it is on the seaward side in the river and has survived all the torrents and floods. The other millstones were built into steps at the entrance to the original Crackington post office at the Manor. The powerhouse and post office are now converted into flats or apartments.

The millpond itself was fed by two leats, one from the stream below Ludon. It flowed behind what was Mascot or Bridge Cottage, under Mill Ball hill and through into the Manor garden. A ram pump was installed in the East Wood, which supplied surrounding farms and the Manor, a masterpiece of engineering at the time. The header tank on top of the hill above Cam Vean supplied water by gravity to Tremoutha, Ludon and the Manor. Down in the Ludon Valley the pump could be heard for decades, like a heart beating in the East Wood. It was a combined effort between my father and George Parnell, well ahead of mains running water. I have kept the map showing the pipework and its route, although there is little evidence of it today, just the remains of the old sluice gate alongside the river in the East Wood. There is a National Trust property

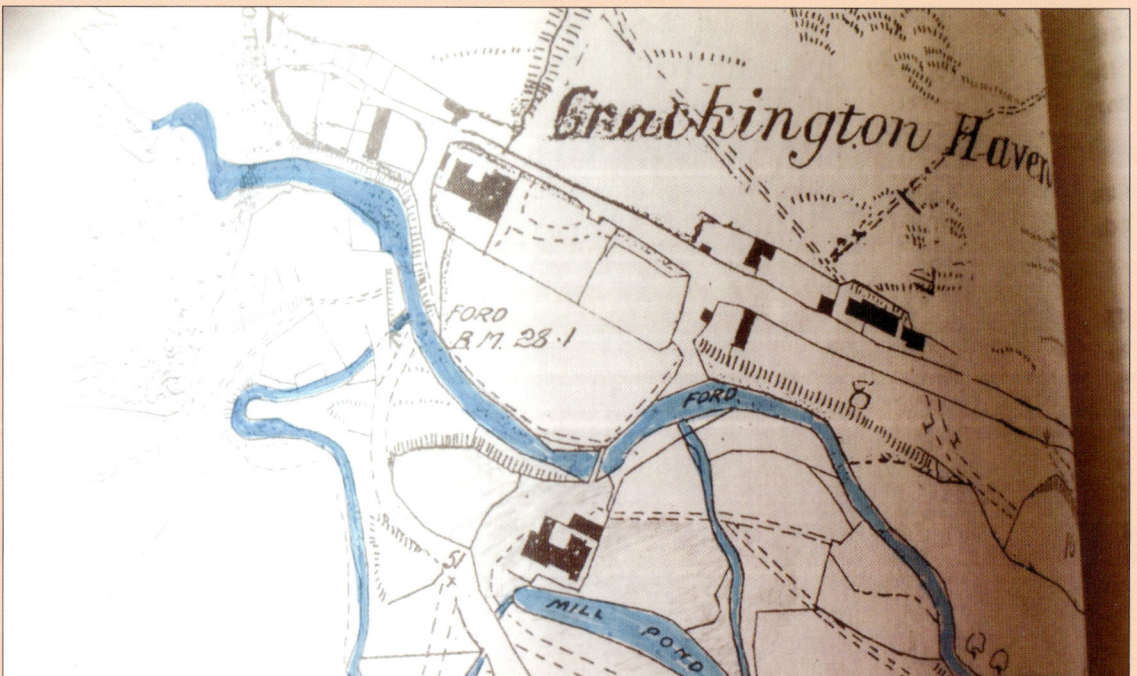

Two fords across the haven

in Sussex called Uppark where I believe there was a similar scheme, which has been preserved and may still be in operation.

Most properties had a well in those days, the Manor had one under its big kitchen floor. The water was pumped into a Butler Sink and was cool and refreshing to drink. The cottage below Ludon on the Tremoutha Road, known as Mascott, later became known as Bridge Cottage. The occupants regularly collected water from a spring through a little gate on the other side of the bridge. When I was younger most people had to carry water and paraffin on a regular basis; children could earn a penny pocket money by helping out. My daughter remembers helping with the washing at Bridge Cottage; it was easier to take it to the stream than carry the water indoors. As for the well water, springs were not contaminated then and everyone became sceptical about drinking the mains water when it was eventually piped into the haven. In the Manor kitchen the mains water was piped to a large sink with a tap used for washing and cleaning. Few trusted the new supply which we feared was full of chemicals and so, for many years, we continued to use the well water pump for drinking. The pendulum has swung in the other direction today as the increase of pollutants in spring water far outweighs the safety of drinking mains water, which is tested regularly.

The other leat flowed from the Coombe Valley where it joined from the weir close to Flanders boundary. The weir is not in existence now, it used to dam river water

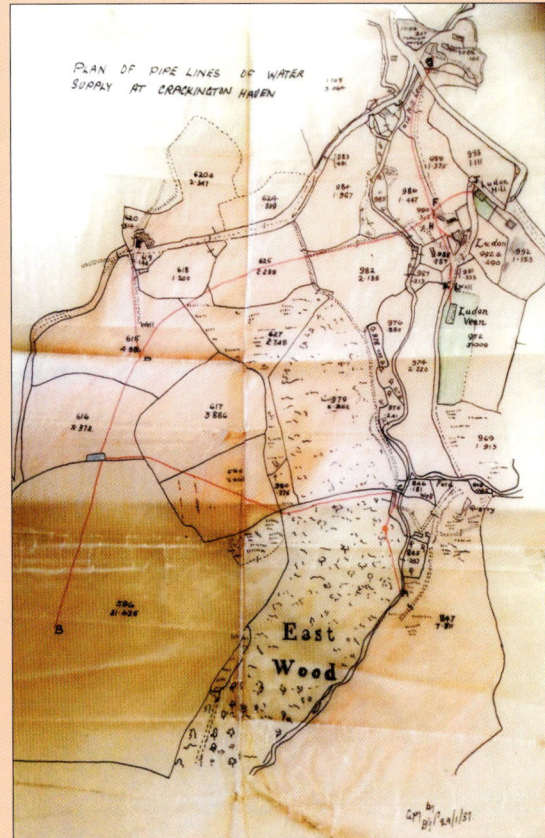

Map of gravity fed water pipes

and channel it through the orchards, alongside the meadow and into the millpond from the eastern end. Maintaining the leat was a routine and arduous task, without regular cleaning it continually silted up and so did the pond it led into. A major cleaning of the millpond required a horse and skoop hired from a farmer. The skoop was ideal since it was designed to transfer soil from the bottom of steep hilly fields back up to the top. The operation to clean the pond required great precision, with the horse being stationed in the meadow beyond with a long chain attached to the skoop. Stopping the horse at the exact spot was vital or it spelt disaster!

Skooping the pond

Maintaining the maximum amount of water in the millpond was essential to the performance of the water-driven generator in the powerhouse below. The water was directed from the pond, through a sluice gate down to the water turbine, which ran an eighty-volt generator. This enabled us to power machinery, including a powerful saw for slicing and cutting wood. My father introduced electricity into the Manor and Manor Cottage long before the main electric supply came to the haven. There were no appliances then, just electric lights which all went out when the water supply got low.

Many local people had the luxury of a radio set. When I was about fourteen years of age I was given the responsibility of charging the accumulators, which folks brought to the powerhouse. I was oiling a shaft on an icy cold day with a long, warm scarf wrapped around my neck when it suddenly caught in the turbine and I was tugged forcefully, the scarf tightening around my throat! I was forever thankful to Johnny Hancock, the passerby who heard my screams and found me lying unconscious in the pit below. He used a penknife to release the scarf, dragged me out of the pit and successfully resuscitated me. I was saved from death by strangulation and it took many weeks to fully recover.

There were hazards and dangers all around you in my younger days, we had plenty of warnings but couldn't be watched all the time. Children grew up very quickly and we were given responsibilities very early in life. I was a typical boy and at four years of age I had a serious accident when I fell backwards from the footbridge into the river. There was a safe fence in place but I managed to squeeze through it. I stretched out to gather some flowers that grew in the river wall, tugging with all my might the plant surrendered unexpectedly and I fell about ten to twelve feet backwards into the river below. I cut my head as it hit the rocks and the scar has remained with me for nearly a century!

In addition to providing us with power and energy the millpond was home to a variety of wildlife. Moorhens nested in the bank and there were fish. Over the years the pond created a source of great entertainment. I was working in the garage one day when someone arrived with a compact outboard motor that needed mending. There was a small wooden boat in the pond at the time and, having completed the task, I gave it a test run. By the time I had fixed the motor on to the boat and fired it up, a queue of eager passengers had arrived on the lawn all excited and keen to experience a joy ride around the pond. All went well on that occasion but when my brother was presented with a handcrafted canoe, covered in canvas, things became tricky. Thrilled with this gift he summoned his friends, Walter Polatch, Tony Sandercock and Norman Pickard to name just a few. One by one they took it in turns to paddle across the pond but not one of them could keep a balance and keeled over into the water. I was fetched from the garage to have a go. All the previous participants were soaked to the skin and drenched through to their underpants, but I was fully confident that I could paddle a canoe across the pond and happily boarded fully clothed. All went well until I reached the middle when the boat began to sway from side to side; the more I tried to correct it

William Thomas Tilley

the worse it became. To the delight of my friends, who were enthusiastically cheering me on, I too ended upside down in the pond. We all had a good ducking and laughed our heads off! Such fun doesn't go unnoticed and it wasn't long before all the family were having a go. By then we were trying to counter balance with weights either side to make it stable but the duckings continued and so did the hilarity!

The millstone

The Millpond

Early Days of Good Motoring

The early 1900s was a time of gradual transition from horse and carriage to the early automobile. At the outbreak of the First World War the British government had ordered a large consignment of artillery harnesses, saddles, ambulances and automobiles from an American company based in Indiana. The Studebaker brothers were producing horse-drawn vehicles, wagons for farming and the military; but by 1902 they were manufacturing motor vehicles, battery operated to begin with and then progressing to petrol engines. From 1903 all motor vehicles were required to have a licence before they were permitted on public roads and, in the early days, someone had to walk out in front with a red flag to warn everyone that a car was coming. There were still a lot of horses and cattle on the roads and they didn't expect to meet a car. I remember when I was a child there were only three cars in the haven; Crackington was a very peaceful place then! My father had purchased a Studebaker Tourer after the First World War. The Studebaker Motor Company was out to build the best vehicle on the road and had gained an excellent reputation for quality and reliability. In those days if you wanted a good car you bought from America and, at the time, they were right-hand drives! The national speed limit remained at 20mph until the 1930s. That was fast! I remember the car was very well made, strong and lasted

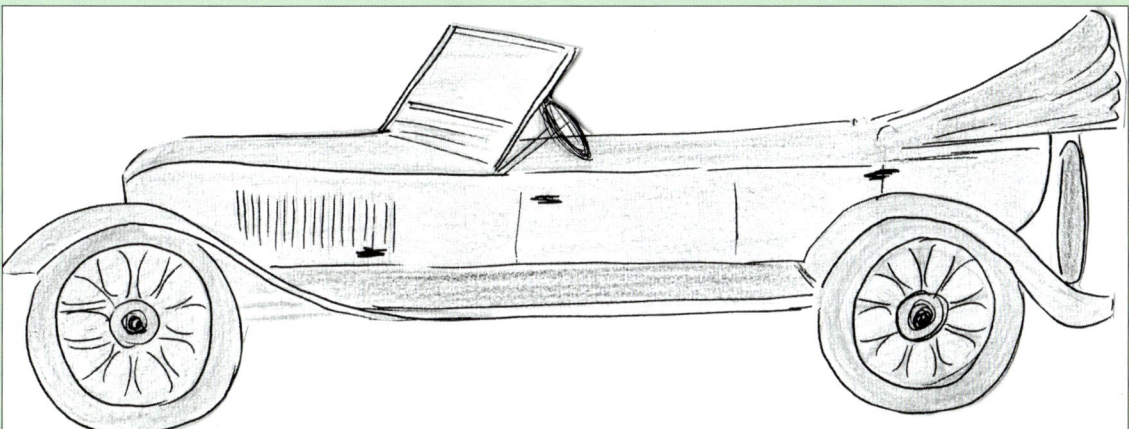

Studebaker

Early automobile

The ford in the haven

Lottie by the footbridge

Water splash

many years. The roads around the parish were rough and the ford in the haven was often impassable. The Studebaker was difficult to drive; it was heavy with wooden spoke wheels and a very long steel chassis, which eventually ended up as the structure for the bridge over the river to the platt. Built as a flat, flood-proof bridge it stood the test of time and survived all floods for about seventy years. My affections for the old Studebaker had transferred to the bridge, it was strong as ever, useful and had found a suitable resting place.

After the Studebaker my father bought an 18hp Crossley with a fabric body, no self-starter and a gate right hand change. I learnt to drive in this and spent hours polishing the aluminium-cased engine. I couldn't wait to be old enough to drive it. The first driving tests were introduced in 1934 so at age seventeen I was one of the first in line. Many failed the test being ill prepared, so my father endeavoured to teach me well in all aspects of town and country driving. Going down a steep hill in Bideford, my father directed me to turn right at the bottom towards the bridge, but suddenly we noticed there was a police officer standing high on a podium in the middle of the road with his hand up. There was little chance of stopping so in order to avoid the officer there was a quick change of instruction to, "Keep left of the officer." My father was in a worried state by now and shouting, "Keep left! Keep left!" The steering was so hard and difficult to swing around the policeman that it felt like I had pulled every ligament in my shoulders. Somehow I managed to leave the bewildered police constable standing in the road. After that experience we practiced every manoeuvre under the sun until I had attained full control. Looking back I could never have imagined how vehicles would change, it's so easy now with power steering, disc brakes and computerised works; no one would want to take a test in the Crossley nowadays! Like all young lads once I had passed my test I thought the world was my oyster. By now my father had acquired a very smart Austin 16 York saloon. One evening I gathered up a group of teenagers for a night out. Bude Pavilion was a newly built venue with a dance café and Saturday night was my chance to demonstrate my newly acquired driving skills. We danced the night away on the new highly polished floor to a 1930s band and merrily bundled into the car to ride home. There was much hilarity and the crowd in the back seat were all singing and swaying about; I held tight to the wheel as the car began to swerve from side to side but, like a lot of overconfident youngsters, I was about to learn a hard lesson. The mood changed when we reached Poundstock and we collided with a post! Not only had I damaged the post but there was some serious damage down one side of the car, so my over confidence turned to shame and dread! My parents were in bed unaware of the consequences of our night out, for me it was a very long sleepless night working out my confessions. Sure

Alfred with the Austin York Saloon

enough in the morning the police arrived. That was the hardest lesson I ever learnt; they say you don't start learning until after the test and that was true.

With lessons learned my father introduced me to the taxi business. There were local, routine jobs and frequent trips to and from the station. Then one day I was asked to pick up a visitor and take her

The early days of good motoring

to Tintagel Castle. It was immediately apparent that she was young and attractive and, as I held the door open for her, she told me she was interested in history. Since it was such a beautiful day, she had booked a taxi to Tintagel. Arriving at our destination I was asked to carry her picnic hamper, which I was more than

willing to do. She chatted away as we walked along, but to be honest she didn't appear to have the slightest interest in the castle, so we found a spot to sit down and enjoy the sun. It wasn't long before we became better acquainted and I felt an arm sliding around my back! There were several visitors around and, before I knew it, she had pulled out a camera and asked a passer-by to take a photo of us together. I enjoyed a good day out and the young lady was planning the next excursion but, unbeknown to me, she had returned her film into the Manor Post Office to be sent for developing. Once returned the photographs were checked to ensure they were developed and sorted for collection. Imagine how I felt when my father showed me the photograph! There we were arm in arm, sat on the grass at Tintagel Castle enjoying a picnic. I was looking forward to her next booking but my father intercepted and was her chauffeur. He wasn't out for long! That all happened before the war. Crackington was a different place, at that point I was a privileged youngster enjoying a perfect life but I didn't know it. I had little comprehension of the wider world or what lay ahead.

St Gennys School

St Gennys School was located at Churchtown, a small tranquil hamlet to the north of Crackington Haven, a perfect setting in the countryside beside the church. Generations of our local families had attended the school. Children living in Crackington Haven had a daily climb of about four hundred feet up over the cliff onto the Barton fields at the top, then through the fields leading down into Churchtown. My sister Lottie and I started school at the age of five and used to climb a path that followed a direct line behind where Thatchways now stands. In those days it was the safest and most direct route for infants. From the Manor our parents would no doubt be able to look up and check on our progress as we

St Gennys School

ascended. We were very young and had instructions not to stray from the path.

I still have vivid memories of the skylarks that sang high in the sky above us, it was one of the highlights of the climb to school. Our headmistress was a great teacher and she enlisted us in the 'Bird Lovers League', the dawn chorus being one of my passions. Not one of us would want to see a bird harmed to this day. My school pal, Reg Wickett, was able to imitate birdsong and sitting at the back of the classroom he would chirp away, our teacher would stop the class so that we could all listen and guess which bird it was singing outside. She struggled to see it and it took some while for her to twig that it was Reg!

There was a weekly gathering of wild flowers and listing the names, my sister excelled in this and usually provided me with some of her surplus to save my bacon. Among other things we were thoroughly educated in, was respect for the countryside and understanding how to care for the environment surrounding us.

I enjoyed reading. Stuart Martin delivered newspapers to the school on his motorbike and sidecar. He was an enthusiastic sportsman and gave us lessons in football before leaving us with the newspapers, which we eagerly read through from the front cover to the back page.

The school building was Victorian with a schoolmaster's house and garden attached. Inside, the schoolroom was heated by means of a black coal stove and, since we attended before the provision of school meals, we would take our pasties to be warmed on the stove in winter. There were no services of course, no electricity or running water so it was all a bit basic. The stove could only heat a small area of the classroom and, on very cold days, we would take breaks outside in order to run up and down to stimulate our circulation! At lunchtime we would run towards the coast, thinking about it now we must have had a long lunch break, or maybe we just ran very fast! We took part in gardening, preparing and planting the schoolhouse vegetable plot. The toilet facilities were in an outside courtyard at the rear of the building on the draughty seaward side.

We left school at age fourteen, today that would not be considered a very good education. I have never been academic; we didn't take exams. The school taught us the basic reading, writing and arithmetic and then we left. Known as "The three Rs." The folks I knew were practical people who learned to use their initiative and work things out for themselves. It takes intelligence and common sense to do that.

Today it seems children are encouraged to streamline their abilities, which results in brilliance in some subjects, but then they're often unable to perform the most menial tasks. Thinking about it, we did it all the other way around!

Many years later
My younger brother was among the first group to experience school dinners. They were prepared in the nearby vicarage wash house, with the vicar's garage converted into a temporary canteen. River water was used to clean vegetables and wash dishes.

Meals were carried to the neighbouring school in a tea chest before the new canteen was built near the school in 1945. Then a modern well-equipped kitchen was built at the school, complete with a sink and tap with access to a well, a toilet and a new black stove. The school meals were all home-cooked by local ladies.

It was the 1950s when I was first contracted to transport children to school from around the parish. An exciting start to the day with narrow lanes, sharp bends and steep hills. My first bus was an 18-

St Gennys school bus

seater; brakes were still very poor and particularly fierce in cold weather. The school milk churn was collected en route from Crannow Farm and stood in the centre isle at the rear of the bus. One exceptionally cold morning with the churn on board, I applied the brakes as usual in order to stop and pick up the next pupil at Tresmorn Lane end. Not accounting for the very cold conditions that day the bus stopped abruptly and, to the delight of the children, the milk churn tipped up spilling its entire contents throughout the bus!

Ann Sandercock was a pupil in the

1940s. She recalls her schooldays walking from Bridge Cottage in the Haven to St Gennys School. At the age of only four this would amount to several miles each day, up some very steep gradients and often in the pouring rain. By the 1940s the post round had improved and was extended with the familiar red vans introduced. If it rained hard there was a possibility of being bundled into the back of a Royal Mail van with the sacks, if the postman had some space. One thing everyone is in agreement about though, our present fitness is most likely due to the strenuous exercise required to attend the local school. And you could guarantee that part of the day's activities would include physical fitness, or country dancing outside in the school playground!

We had our fair share of disasters and sad times; any accident would have a dramatic effect on the whole community. In the 1950s a young pupil strayed from the path and fell from the Penkenna. I remember the description of a young boy wearing short grey trousers, white shirt and a knitted pullover. As the parents gathered in panic on the beach there was nothing that could be done to save him. It was a terrible shock and something that you could never forget.

I was away serving in the army during the war but my younger brother William, known as Roy, often spoke about his schooldays. Being a young lad it must have seemed very exciting as evacuees from London, Plymouth and elsewhere attended the St Gennys School. It was impossible to accommodate everyone in the small classroom, so part of the neighbouring vicarage was turned into a temporary school. Different accents were just one of the minor issues at the time, with no television and very little radio, the children hadn't been exposed to the various dialects. From cockney to Cornish the problem must have been easily overcome as many evacuees forged long-term friends and relationships. Most have returned to visit since the war and there are families who made Crackington their permanent home.

It was during the school dinner break that a German bomber was seen circling over the sea, close to the cliff near the school. Roy and his friends ran to the cliff edge to watch as it dropped a bomb, trying to hit a small Dutch boat loaded with coal. The boat became stranded on shingle and her crew of nine scrambled ashore. The cargo of coal burned for four days. My sister Lottie took good care of the crew and they later presented her with a tea set in appreciation.

An outbreak of chickenpox guaranteed a long break from school. The incubation period was deemed to be three weeks, therefore anyone in contact with the disease could not attend school. The sisters fell ill one after the other so Roy had an extended holiday that year and also managed to escape the chickenpox!

It was recorded that in 1895 there was severe weather in St Gennys from January through to March. The school was closed for three weeks due to an epidemic of whooping cough and influenza, which affected every household in the parish.

There were various schoolmasters over the century including Mr Bell, Mr Cook, Mr Tonkin, Miss Wellington, Mrs Lane, Mr and Mrs Crabb, Mr and Mrs Bloomer, Mrs Francis and, my own uncle, William Rundle Ward, who unfortunately died in

Pupil	Father	Address
Mary Tilley	Thomas Tilley	Flanders
John Goodman	Richard Goodman	Congdons
Laura Sandercock	Thomas Sandercock	Sweets
Elizabeth Sandercock	William Sandercock	Hallagather
Thirza Sandercock	Thomas Sandercock	Sweets
William Tilley	Thomas Tilley	Flanders
Alfred Tilley	Thomas Tilley	Flanders
William Ward	John HP Ward	Bay Park
Annie Sandercock	Richard Sandercock	Flanders
Esther Kate Ward	John HP Ward	Bay Park
Richard Tilley	James Tilley	Hill Road
Emily G Tilley	James Tilley	Hill Road
Winifred Tilley	James Tilley	Hill Road

Example of pupils registered in the 1800s

St Gennys class in 1895

the prime of his life. There is a memorial erected in his memory in the form of an archway over the main gate to the Brockhill cemetery on the south side.

St Gennys School closed in the 1970s – it was the end of an era! Attending the school was a family tradition and future generations would now be taken to a neighbouring parish. The canteen was demolished and the school has been converted into a residential dwelling.

It is still very good exercise and I can recommend a hike up over the cliff and across the Barton fields to Churchtown. If you hear some singing and look up you may even see a skylark!

St Gennys School over the cliff

Photograph of the school reunion in 2002 which includes some of the pupils who attended the school in the 1940s and 1950s Clive Tilley, Roger Teague, Mervyn Northcott, Julia Tilley, Alan Sandercock, Christopher Biscombe, Rex Ward, Thomas Bunney, Jennifer Northcott, Ann Rogers, Margaret Mason, Elaine Boney, Ann Sandercock, Norah Trewin, Christine Bloomer, Carol Sandercock, Yvonne Sandercock, John Rogers

St Gennys school at Churchtown

Mineshop

Cornwall is renowned for its rich mineral resources; the economy of the county depended on the mining industry for centuries. Tin, copper, lead, manganese, iron, silver, uranium and wolfram were all mined in Cornwall before the war. Since then demand declined and the old mines and engine houses have now become landmarks around the county, making interesting attractions for visitors. St Austell is still famous for the production of Kaolin or China Clay, the high mountains of waste and water-filled open pits have become known as the Cornish Alps. There is a granite quarry at De Lank on Bodmin Moor and, at Delabole, the open slate quarry has been in operation since the 1200s. The main wolfram mine at Castle-an-Dinas, four miles north of St Austell, closed in 1958. Minerals such as arsenic were mined along with wolfram, which is better known as tungsten today. It's incredibly dense and, being so heavy, it was the perfect material for bullets and

Mineshop

missiles. Its true value and strength was not discovered until the late 19th century and, in later times, it was found to have all the properties required for the filaments in a light bulb. The areas around Crackington are mineral rich, there have been discoveries and surveys over the years along the coastal areas at Dizzard and Cleave, north of Crackington. In the valley to the east of the haven, between Tremayna and Middle Crackington, there was a working mine at Mineshop, which

Lovers Walk: Footpath through to Congdons & Mineshop, one of the old postal routes through the woods

many people are familiar with. Like most Cornish mines it is redundant and covered in. Mineshop has been developed into a holiday complex.

At Mineshop, the old mineshaft produced minerals including zinc, silver, lead and wolfram. Over the years it has been surveyed by various miners, including the Camborne School of Mines. I understand the shaft to be about thirteen fathoms, or up to twenty-three metres deep. It has had its fair share of casualties.

The captain of the mine, who came from Bere Alston in the Tamar Valley, fell to his death from a ladder in 1835. It was a dangerous operation and, although the mine contained minerals, it was not practical or economical.

There was a blacksmith at Mineshop where my uncle worked as a young lad. I'm not sure what he had in mind but the blacksmith, Albert Cory, decided to experiment with making a rocket! My uncle Fred worked with Albert at the blacksmith's shop and experienced the launch first-hand. Albert filled the hub of a cartwheel with dynamite, laid out on the floor he tamped the dynamite down with an iron bar. The experiment came to an unexpected halt when the cartwheel exploded firing the iron bar with immense force through the roof of the building! Apparently the iron bar was never recovered and Albert claimed he'd put the first rocket into space! After his apprenticeship with Albert, my uncle Alfred Tilley emigrated to America.

At St Gennys school many of the boys had steel hoops to play with; not having one myself I went to visit Albert after school one day. Albert agreed to make me a super model complete with a leader but, unbeknown to me, he sent my father the bill for seven shillings and sixpence, a lot of money in those days. I have erased what was said from my memory but I do remember the excitement we had rolling the hoops from the top of the hills down to the beach. I hasten to add there were no cars in those days!

It may be of interest to know that we found some large heavy chunks of

A view from Starlight garden showing the Middle Coombe valley towards Congdons

The annual hill trial at Mineshop

wolfram when excavating to install the petrol tanks by the shop, now the Cabin Café beside the beach. These days people have so much leisure time on their hands that a café is far more profitable. If times get hard they could always start digging!

There is a trial hill at Mineshop where sports enthusiasts enjoy the challenge of driving up a steep, rocky track. The water splash ford at the bottom of the hill adds to the mud. Held on Easter Saturday the trial has been an annual event for decades. My brother Roy built a sports car from scratch, which he entered one year. On quieter days the trial hill is a very pleasant woodland walk across the ford via a footbridge, then climbing to Middle Crackington at the top.

Lovers Lane: Cart track to Starlight and footpath to Lovers Walk

Pottery sold at Crackington Post Office

World War 2

Alfred December 1939

We were gathered together as a family when World War 2 was declared; the announcement given by the Prime Minister of the time, Neville Chamberlain. There were some very mixed feelings amongst us, as the First World War had not been forgotten. It was a sobering time for my parents, my uncle Alfred had gone to war just twenty-two years earlier and, at that time, he was in the prime of life in his twenties. His grave is in France, somewhere among the many thousands who lost their lives in the Battle of the Somme. Young men were forced out of mud-filled trenches to go over the top, knowing they had little hope of survival. Horses were taken away from the farms and we heard some gruelling experiences from those who survived horrendous ordeals. Millions had died in the last war and no one wanted to go through another. All eyes were on me, but I knew I was not cut out to be a soldier. There was a campaign to recruit volunteers and I had little choice, as I was a fit 22-year-old with a driving licence. So in December 1939 I joined the Royal Army Service Corp as a volunteer driver. My young brother William Roy was only 8-years-old and attended St Gennys School, while my three sisters lived at home. I suddenly had a wake-up call and found out what life was really like! Up until that point I had lived comfortably surrounded by a happy and loving family. I couldn't have asked for better parents, there was always an abundance of wholesome home-cooked food on the table. I was happy and content living in an idyllic peaceful location, working at home with my father in the

An emotional farewell

Manor and on the farm. All my friends and relations were here in this rural community and I had never had the reason to venture far from home, but now all this was going to change dramatically.

I was in the army for a very long six-and-a-quarter years. Leaving home I boarded the train at Otterham Station for a slow, tiring journey to Margate, where I had no idea what I was in for! It was past midnight when I arrived and I was taken to a freezing cold building packed with other volunteers. It was midwinter and there was no heat, the only space to lay my straw bed was in front of an open fireplace where the wind whistled through and down the chimney. I was exhausted and shaking with extreme cold; I have never been so cold in all my life! I spent the night realising what a privileged life I had enjoyed up until now. Without a doubt this was a big changing point!

I well remember the first time on the rifle range. If you were a good marksman then there was a strong possibility of being transferred to the infantry as a sniper. I had volunteered as a driver, prepared and confident to drive under whatever difficult circumstances presented themselves. The targets were quite large and anyone with a steady hand and the aid of telescopic sights could easily get somewhere near the target, but I was not particularly interested in becoming a dead hero! I soon realised that being a good soldier was not necessarily in ones best interest. With my late uncle and survival in mind, I carefully aimed the bullets towards the outer circle of the target! Thankfully I was assigned to a troop carrying company and, after brief training, I became responsible for a two-ton Bedford truck. On the 25th January 1940 I was put on a troop carrying ship to Cherbourg in France. First time abroad but this was no pleasure trip. The boat was cramped and we were packed like sardines in a tin, every inch of space was taken. It was not an easy assignment either, escorting soldiers through France in night-time convoys, travelling under the cover of darkness with only a pinpoint light for guidance. There were many pitfalls and ditches to negotiate in a strange country and it was altogether a difficult and dangerous mission.

By the spring of 1940 the German troops had advanced so we had to get out of France immediately. Our troops were desperately needed back home to defend against a Nazi invasion. Thousands of men were trapped on the beaches of Dunkirk waiting to be evacuated. Small boats were ferrying men to the larger passenger ships waiting out in the sea. I was with a group of men along the coast at Digue, injured and nursing a fractured arm. I have heard it said that I was flown back to England as a result of my injury but that was not the case. We escaped, pushed out to sea in a small rowing boat with an outboard motor. Chugging out across the channel, we were sitting ducks, targets expecting to be shot or machine-gunned at sea! The weather was favourable and miraculously we reached the safety of Dover unharmed. From there we had to report to Aldershot that we were still alive. Things were pretty awful then. Military hospitals were not pleasant places, but I was counting my blessings to be back in England. After being admitted to hospital for a few weeks treatment I was prepared for the next assignment, which was at Leamington Spa. I was provided with a BSA motorbike and joined a newly formed Traffic Control

The first Crackington post office

Company. I was assigned to direct and navigate convoys of troops since there were no signposts. All the time Germans were flying around overhead. Coventry was bombed while I was there, you could hear the deafening noise and the night sky was so bright you could see to read a newspaper from miles away. While stationed at Leamington Spa I was able to assist at the Longbridge factory in Birmingham, which was a place buzzing with activity. Life at that time was full of uncertainty; the war seemed set to last and there were many bombings and casualties. My sisters sent postcards from Crackington Post Office where they were keeping busy. They told me that Plymouth had been bombed and the resulting glow in the sky could be seen from as far as North Cornwall!

Postcard from Crackington

be my best man. I met Martha in Cornwall many years before the war, her elder sister Ruth had married a local St Gennys man, Frank Tape. As a young girl Martha had

The German boat wrecked at Tremoutha Haven

It was during this time that I took leave in order to get married, something that we planned for after the end of the war, but there was no end in sight. Travelling was difficult so my family were not present; my good friend Reg Wickett was able to

been a frequent visitor to Crackington and we had struck up a romance, but all our future plans had been pushed aside by the war. Like many young women Martha was now working in a munitions factory. London was under fire and her brother had been killed by a bomb in a direct hit. The munitions factory was a dangerous place to work and, sure enough, my fiancée was involved in an accident when a device fell on her foot and turned it septic. That incident resulted in an amputation of the toe, but could have been worse as the infection had spread. There was no wedding dress or frills, the ceremony was a simple affair at Martha's home in London before returning for duty. On occasions Martha was able to get the train from London and we spent some time together. We danced to the music of Vera Lynn, whose voice uplifted the spirit of the troops all through those difficult years. Martha continued working in the factory until she returned one day to find

Alfred & Martha on their wedding day

Telegrams from Crackington Post Office

their home had been demolished by a bomb. The family had a really tough time in London, they had lost everything and spent many nights in damp air-raid shelters. In fact my nephew was born during an air raid! Doodlebugs flew over exceptionally fast and you could see the jet flame behind it – you never knew where it would drop. My father-in-law was a volunteer fireman during the war, which was a very precarious occupation and kept him busy. He had a wacky sense of humour. When someone commented about how fast the Doodlebugs flew, his answer was "So would you if you had that flame firing out of your backside!" You needed a good sense of humour to survive all that. My mother-in-law kept him in order. She had been born and raised in a military family in Bangalore in India and

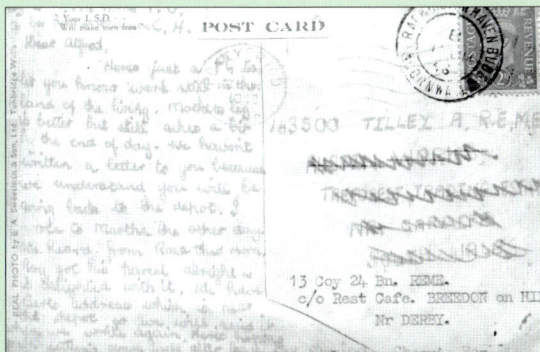
Card from home

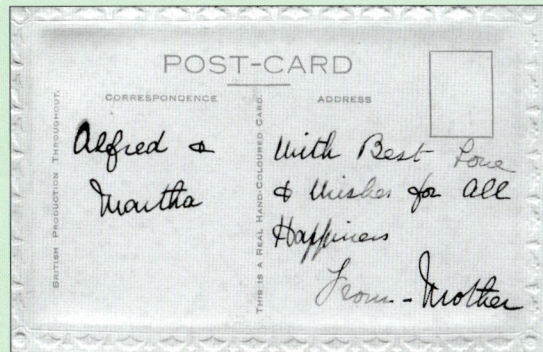
Wedding card from Mother

returned to live in England in her twenties. It must have been tough but she had a large family and managed everything with military precision. One of my brothers-in-law was a butcher and had a very large old refrigerator; on occasions there was no time to get to an air-raid shelter so everyone packed into the fridge! Martha, realising she was expecting our first baby, went to live with my family at Crackington Manor where she found safety and was welcomed with open arms.

The next transfer took me to the headquarters, a large house with only about a dozen men. There were offices for the major, the commanding officer and the captain. Plus we had the luxury of our own cook! I was there for some time and kept busy with dispatch riding in Birmingham, Hereford and all over the Midlands. Later I became chauffeur to the lieutenant, who was based in the headquarters at Kidderminster. I drove the adjutant all around the Midlands in an Austin 10 Tourer, which was the best job so far. One thing for sure, I certainly got to know my way around and see all the different areas; there were no signposts of course so you needed to be a good map reader. Eventually I had the chance to transfer from the RASC and join the newly formed Royal Electrical and Mechanical Engineers. I was sent to Walthamstow College for a course in mechanical engineering, which was a positive and valuable experience and of great interest to me. I was eager to learn everything I could and grasped the opportunity for

Martha & Alfred during the war

further training at Newbury, before being posted to Donington Park. Along with a dozen or so other men we were billeted at Bredon, which was the regimental and military training ground. Saturday morning training sessions were held in a disused quarry, where Sten guns were issued; the golden rule in the army being to take good care of your weapons. Unbeknown to me someone had plugged a sycamore bud in the barrel of my gun and it had caused a reaction to the metal. No matter how hard I tried I could not clean it. An inspection was due and I would be in for big trouble! An unexpected turn of events meant that when the time came we were ordered to hand in the Stens and collect new rifles from the quartermaster's stores. I never knew who'd interfered with my gun, although I had my suspicions.

During my term in the army I found some of my superiors were real gentlemen, who earned great respect and looked out for their men. While, I'm sad to say, others were downright irresponsible, looking for ways to exert their power and intent on creating trouble. You had to be watching your back all the time! At Donington Park we worked hard repairing military vehicles before moving on to the task of making them watertight before the invasion.

Of all the challenges we faced I never expected to be threatened by a bull! During our time at Donington Park we had to sleep in bunk beds in a converted barn. I presumed the farmer was not very happy about the arrangement as he insisted on keeping a temperamental

Martha with Lottie and Roy at the Manor

Friesian bull loose in the yard. This was our only means of access and I knew enough about bulls to know that this one could not be trusted! The farmer declared it harmless even though he always carried a pike when he was anywhere near it. He obviously found it amusing as we sped hastily across the yard, petrified and with one eye on the bull. One day, approaching with the usual caution, we noticed there was no sign of it. It was of no surprise to learn later that it had attacked the farmer! A cattle truck had taken the bull away and that was the last we saw of both the bull and the farmer. This incident convinced me that if I ever returned to civilian life I would definitely not return to farming!

Traffic Control Company at Leamington Spa

My eldest son was born whilst I was serving in the army. A significant event for any couple but I found it very difficult to get leave to see him. Martha was living at Crackington with my family and, when the time came for the birth, things weren't straightforward and she had to be taken to a hospital in Looe, as Plymouth had been bombed. I managed to get sufficient leave just to see them both for an hour or so. It took all day to travel to Cornwall and then my father was not permitted to use his car beyond ten miles, so I had to get another train. Looe is over on the other coast and not the most accessible place, so by the time I arrived I was as exhausted as my wife! After a brief visit I had to make the return journey for duty the next day.

It must have been very strange for Martha living at home with my parents and family. Everything was a new experience; she was now living in a remote area of Cornwall that was very different to life in London! The Manor was full to the brim, every room taken with family and evacuees, but I knew she was in good hands. She had a new baby to care for but there would be plenty of help. My sister Monica had married by this time and was also living at the Manor with her husband John. Their eldest son Trevor was born there so there would be two young baby boys. My sisters welcomed her into the home and my mother introduced Martha to the traditions of Cornish cookery. By the time I had eventually left the army she had mastered the art of making a good pasty.

When the war ended there were celebrations all over the country for VE

Day. I heard a lot about it. I was in Germany and I wasn't celebrating as it would be another year before I could return home. In Crackington an evacuee had let off a firework from Penquite. Gorse burns easily and it immediately set the cliff on fire! As you can imagine the fire spread rapidly along Penkenna and the whole community had to rally around to fight it, as it threatened nearby houses and thatched cottages. It eventually stopped at the gulley by Thatchways – water made the break!

As for the invasion of Germany, history has provided some graphic details of events both before and after the invasion.

Some people like to talk about these things but I prefer not to recall those days. However, I will tell you this much; I was in Germany for one year after the invasion and the country was torn to pieces – a demolition site! The people were in a desperate state, only just existing. They were to be pitied! I visited concentration camps and saw the gas chambers although, thankfully, I didn't see the worst of it. Suffice it to say, it was absolutely ghastly and you could see and smell what went on there. Our company was then directed to Hamburg where we lived out of a truck, hidden away and covered in camouflage. It was rough. Very rough! I

Family at home

was provided with a car and assignment of workshop control, supervising and inspecting the engineering works. Then one day my superior was struggling to load fuel into his vehicle and I was ordered to assist and get into his car to help unload at the other end. I didn't trust the man but I had to obey orders; you couldn't argue with your superiors! My instincts were confirmed when he refused to stop at a Russian checkpoint, he put his foot down on the accelerator and drove flat out! I was horrified as we found ourselves under gunfire, bullets flew at the car as he raced on, but he got away with it. Unbeknown to me he was supplying farmers with fuel while everyone I knew was under tight restrictions and couldn't have any. Anyway, I survived that ordeal and from then on he kept well out of my way. As I said before you met all types. I kept busy with my own assignment and I found the people in Germany were the same as people anywhere, various different characters with their families struggling to survive! We made some good acquaintances and in time I was able to learn enough of the language to communicate well. That all happened a very long time ago but I can still remember some of the German language to this day.

My father-in-law was a volunteer firefighter in London during the war

Post War, Trade and Tragedy

Youths usually have decisions to make as they grow up, a choice of which path to follow. During the war years many of those decisions were made for us, like it or not! The war changed everything and everyone. Life at home in Crackington had changed. I yearned to get home and establish myself into a normal life and provide for my family. It is unthinkable what soldiers and civilians had endured, tens of millions died in one of the biggest conflicts ever. Many did not return or were left scarred for life. I never want to see another war again! Those of us grateful to be alive were desperate to return home to civilian life but there had been a complete change on the home front!

Even after the war rationing continued with coupons for what was considered the basic essentials. We are an island nation and the German submarines had tried their best to starve us by destroying cargo and supply ships. It took a long time to establish the food production again and butchers could only sell what had been issued to them. It was 1953 before the sugar rationing finally ended and, a year later, for meat and other items to become available. I now had a wife and son to support, my father had been taken ill and my mother had a lot of responsibility on her hands. My sisters Lottie, Eileen and Monica worked flat out in the Manor; my brother Roy was a good all-rounder. I often wonder how things would be if there had been no war. I suppose things would have gradually altered over time, but as it was there were dramatic changes. Our beaches had been barricaded with ugly defences and concrete tank traps, now at last we saw those reminders of war buried under. In fact they were put to good use by helping combat erosion along the beach head. No one wanted to be constantly reminded of those dreadful times. The beach was open again and a return to freedom and peace along our beautiful coast was applauded. Today there are a few remains of the war, the old German U-boat embedded in the rocks at Tremoutha, some coastal lookouts around the coast and war memorials.

Farming had completely changed, horses had been exchanged for tractors. Horses had been in demand through both wars and it was horsemeat that had fed the troops. The first tractors were large heavy machines with iron wheels and not suited to the steep hilly fields around

Crackington, but after the Second World War grey Fergusons or red David Browns were becoming popular.

Prior to the war there had been no restrictions on building, there was an acute shortage of building materials between the wars though. It was a case of using what was on hand. I built some kitchen units from driftwood, washed clean and smooth; kitchen units were a new concept then. It never ceases to amaze me what was accomplished with so little and no machinery. In the mid 1940s the Town and Country Planning Act came into effect. Prior to the planning system most people generally built with consideration and common sense. The old and historic houses we see around us were, for the most part, well constructed and thoughtfully designed. Old buildings have stood the test of time and, by using local materials, they have sat attractively within the natural landscape. Many of the quaint Cornish cottages were spoilt when a grant became available which encouraged the occupants to raise their roofs and install bigger windows. Nowadays building materials are readily available and identical houses pop up like mushrooms! Row after row of houses all the same. Some of the best agricultural land, whole vistas of green pastures disappear virtually overnight! We appreciate that families need homes, but there is little sympathy or consideration to the character of the area. Crackington has its own unique stone and slate, you still see walls capped with spar stone, slate flagstones and other local features. Being a coastal area many dwellings were built as

second homes. It's become controversial in recent times but it never was a problem, in fact we regarded them as neighbours and friends. It brought employment to a rural area as local tradesmen cared for and maintained the properties, the ones I have known maintained their homes well. I'm sure the council tax paid into the system is welcomed, while the services rendered in return are very seldom used. Divorce used to be unheard of, families used to stick together under the same roof even if they had a bust up, so we didn't need so many extra homes in years gone by.

By the 1950s oil lamps were discarded in favour of electricity. We already had electric lights from the water-powered generator at the Manor, but I was now able to wire the house for mains power and electric sockets. The electricity company was based in Bude and offered to wire up homes for around £50 per household – if my memory serves me correctly. This was the beginning of a new era and gradually wireless sets, electric ovens, fridges and a multitude of other gadgets were introduced. Most homes had piped water installed, all dug by hand. Also flush toilets and a kitchen sink. I remember the telephone cables being laid through St Gennys, when the company were working just above Trethew they failed to take into account the steep incline. My uncle Stephen had a number of large chicken houses in the field, probably about thirty feet long. The huge reel of cable took off and hurled down across the field, clean through a chicken house from one end and out the other. The reel kept going, gathering speed as it rolled down the valley towards Congdons Bridge.

You have to move with the times and, after the dismal years of war, people wanted a change in their circumstances and more freedom. I was offered a lucrative job, teaching mechanical engineering. There were many times when I wondered if I should have accepted a job with a salary and security or return to the Longbridge factory, but as things turned out after the war it became a hot bed of unrest and strikes. I wanted to sever all ties with the wartime and I was pleased to return home to work. My younger brother had joined the army later and also declined promotion for secure work after the war. Finally, as adults we were given a choice, our decision was not to take the easy option! Demobbed, meant leaving the army with very little and it was going to be a real struggle! It seemed like we lived from hand to mouth for a very long time and I had to start from scratch! This was the reality of living in a remote coastal area in Cornwall. Crackington Haven at that time was exceptionally quiet and off the beaten track.

The ford in Crackington was unsuitable for traffic, it was often impassable due to

Letter from the Welcome Home Committee

heavy rain or flooding. More and more people were getting cars and the need for a road bridge was on the agenda. There was much discussion about road improvements and where the bridge would cross. At Congdons Bridge, from the Manor across to Little Pen where the old ford crossed, or in its current location? My father felt the current road bridge would restrict the flow of water in a flood situation and would be better raised and situated further back upstream. It is difficult to visualise anything different now, the bridge is part of the haven but there are two rivers converging under two bridges, which does create a bottleneck in storms and high water. Many times I have seen a stormy sea wash up onto the road and across the bridge, the rivers are forced to back up in the valleys. The new road

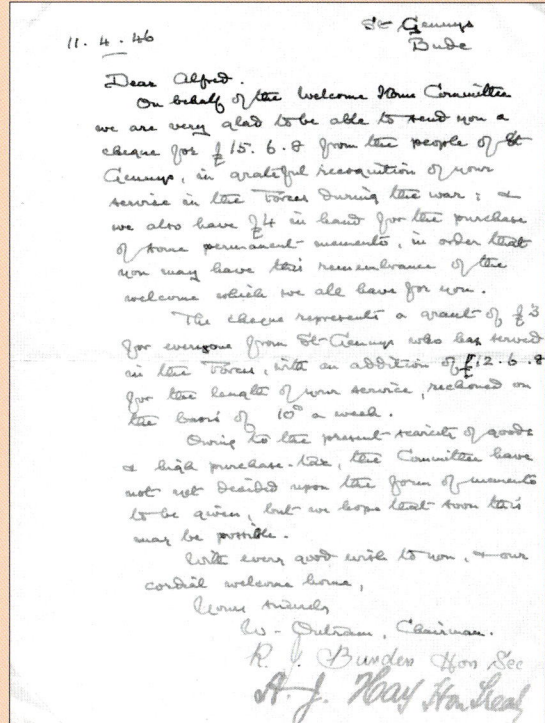

bridge was constructed in the 1950s, road improvements were made and we could never have imagined such an increase in vehicles. From just three cars when I was young to a full car park and constant traffic travelling up and down Pentreath and Mill Ball hills! The roads were never built to take this volume of traffic! Single track highways with some sharp narrow bends, potential landslides and verge parking make it a very dangerous approach to the haven. In years gone by if you had a car it was kept in a garage, during the 1950s visitors could use one of the wooden garages in the car park.

My father kindly let us use the Manor Cottage rent-free until I could get a business established. The college had taught me well in all aspects of engineering and I was grateful for that. My grandparents went to live with my Aunt Bessie and Uncle Will Sandercock at Wooda Farm. Bessie (Mary Elizabeth) was my father's younger sister and they were very close to my parents. We had a few pieces of basic utility furniture to furnish Manor Cottage and I had a vice on a bench with a few essential tools to get started. The garage gradually became useful. More people were getting cars that needed repairs and this led to the natural progression of the petrol station. It was, however, a struggle to obtain the planning permission. Folks were crying out for service stations, cars didn't go far on a gallon and petrol stations were few and far between. There was another application submitted at the same time on the north side of the bridge. Our planning was finally approved for a petrol station

on the south side. It was considered that had the station been on the north side this would block the scenery up the valley and, with visibility reduced by Coombe Barton corner, the access was considered dangerous. Today it is the main car park with vehicles coming and going all day and night. I don't think there is a view up the valley any more! Our planning conditions required us to keep the bank and vegetation cut back, providing a visual splay for vehicles approaching from

the corner at the bottom of Mill Ball hill to the entrance of the forecourt. The next task was to excavate large pits and install the tanks, which was hard labour all dug by hand. The ground was hard and it was during this time that I found the lumps of heavy wolfram! My nephew was staying with us from Kensington in London; free from city life he was always keen to participate in all the projects. I had finally finished digging the pit and, after laying a foundation of fresh cement in the bottom, I covered over the top with planks of wood. Aware of the danger I tested the planks by walking across them to ensure they were stable. The next thing I knew, my nephew followed with enthusiasm. With his thin arms outstretched to maintain his balance, he lost his confidence halfway and, with arms flapping up and down, he flipped over sideways down through the planks and into the sloppy wet cement below! There was no health and safety back then, we did our best to keep everyone safe but accidents did happen.

I lacked equipment in the garage and this presented hazards. I had a nasty accident one day when I was underneath the engine of a car, the jacks supporting it failed and the vehicle crashed onto my chest. I was alone in the garage and thought this could be fatal! On this occasion it was my son who heard me shout and came to my rescue. I have had a few scrapes. I had an accident while using the acetylene, a flammable gas that I used for welding metal. I have a deep scar in the temple to this day from the burn of the colourless flame. In time I built myself a drive-on vehicle ramp out in the backyard, another project but it proved to be invaluable and much safer.

We had increased our family, both my younger son and daughter were born at home in a room overlooking the sea. They arrived in a hurry and I had to abandon my work to become the midwife. One was born head first in a bedpan, while the other was more considerate and waited for Dr Hillier to arrive from Boscastle. The

Martha with her infant daughter

children grew up following the family tradition, a hike up over the cliff to school and helping out with the business.

The holiday trade had begun and it was all hands on deck during the summer months. The season was much shorter then, beginning with the first few visitors at Easter and then it was a case of making hay while the sun shone, because everyone completely disappeared in September. We were up early and there was a constant buzz of activity from morning until we fell into bed exhausted at night. Many visitors arrived by train at Otterham Station and we met them in a taxi. Nearly everyone offered accommodation in those days, the family would have to make space as every available room was needed. The Manor was full of guests; the chalets up in the valley were in demand and occupied with visitors. Children had chores: cleaning, feeding animals, collecting eggs and so forth. Martha served cream teas in both the cottage and garden. By now we had the garage, taxi business, a petrol filling

TILLEY'S

MANOR GARAGE
CRACKINGTON HAVEN

—

TAXI

MINI-COACH

COACH HIRE

—

Phone
ST. GENNYS 244

station and visitors booking coach tours around Cornwall. As for breakdowns and call outs, it was not unusual for people to stall on the hill due to the steep gradient – not being used to having to select a lower gear! In the earlier days radiators would boil and brakes got hot. Petrol was served, wound up using handpumps and a drip pad. We offered to check the oil, tyres and

wash the windscreen. The farm provided an abundance of milk, cream, butter, eggs and much more. My mother cooked all day. My sisters were post office assistants as well as everything else. Everyone worked flat out. The holiday trade was an essential means of earning a living over a relatively short space of time; after the end of September it was very unusual to see a visitor until the following Easter.

Trade and Tragedy

Living so close to the beach there was a demand for buckets and spades, surfboards, kites and all kinds of beach goods. Even though we weren't on the map as it were, the haven was becoming more popular with the same visitors returning year after year. The beach gradually became a recreational facility and the little petrol station kiosk began to expand into a beach shop. We used to hire out deckchairs and surfboards, which often got left on the beach. It was an end of day chore for the children to collect them up and bring them back, more often than not this entailed a dip as the tide would have come in and the deckchairs and surfboards would be floating about on the waves.

Traders began calling on a regular basis, Mr Orchard from Week St Mary was a general outfitter. He had an Austin 16 packed full of haberdashery. The car was weighed down and bulging from the large case strapped on the roof to the footwells inside. At every house he would unpack what seemed to be the entire contents of his suitcases. If you didn't buy something from the first few, then he would continue to unpack until you were snowed under with vests, tea towels, sheets, towels and suchlike. His favourite trick to keep you interested were his silky knickers. He would whisk them out in glee and hold them up high to reveal 'Never on Sunday' embroidered across the front! I'm not sure how many ladies in the parish had a pair of these because they seemed reasonably priced, but sometimes the only way out was to buy something, anything, and give him a cup of tea before he finally left. He was smart in a very tight-fitting suit, a stocky man and we were all fascinated to see how he managed to get into his packed car. There wasn't an inch to spare! Procter and Kent from Launceston were ironmongers with pots and pans, nails, screws, paints and all kinds of useful tools and necessities. Ferrets from Boscastle were the travelling grocers, Foleys came from Launceston. Stuart Martin delivered daily newspapers and Fred Bunt brought fish from Port Isaac. There was an Indian man called Nan Sing who arrived on a bike complete with turban; no one knew where he came from but he carried an array of spectacular silks and colourful embroidered materials. Everyone made their own clothes in those days, but I never saw anyone dressed in this finery! It was unfortunate timing when Nan Sing called on Martha one morning as she was exceptionally busy. It was one of those days when there was so much to do and like the cow's tail, she was all behind! As for cooking, the old range fire had gone out! Sometimes everything goes wrong, the range in Manor Cottage had seen better days and it was a struggle to light at

the best of times. Martha, in desperation, picked up an old cloth from the garage and sprinkled it with paraffin. She placed the cloth under the kindling and set a match to it just as Nan Sing approached the door with his wares. In spite of Martha's apology for lack of time, he persisted and continued on with his usual repertory, unpacking the fabulous array of silks, scarves and a flamboyant display all over the kitchen floor; when, suddenly,

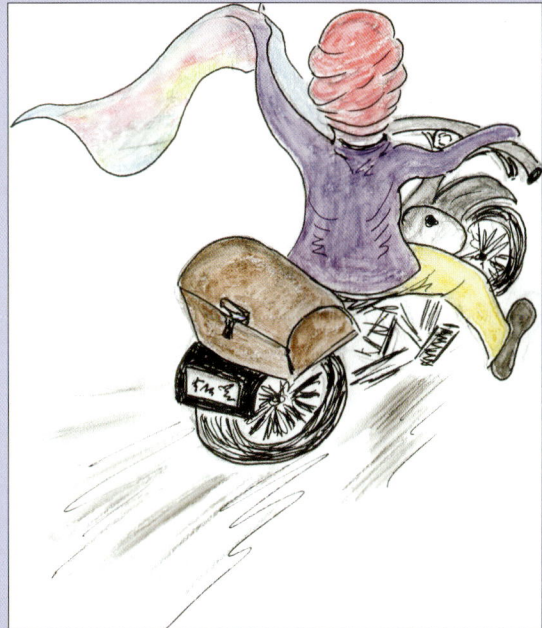

there was an almighty bang! It sounded like an explosion in the kitchen and poor Nan Sing must have thought it was a gunshot. He swiftly grabbed his wares and flew off on his bike up the hill with a trail of brightly coloured material flying out from behind! Meanwhile the kitchen range was alight with flames leaping about two feet high! The cloth and paraffin had exploded big time! We never saw Nan Sing again, but after that escapade we installed a new Aga cooking range.

The local policeman lived at Wainhouse Corner, he used to cycle around on his bicycle. Thinking about it now I suppose he didn't have much to do. No one ever locked their door, the thought of crime never entered our heads. He was on good terms with everyone and regularly called into the Sandercocks at Bridge Cottage for his tot of sloe gin. That was in the earlier days and how we took it all for granted; we never carried keys and nothing had to be locked. A door key was a big, heavy object, several inches long, which would never fit in your pocket. Today everything has to be locked and bolted, such a shame as keys are a perfect nuisance. Just imagine the local policeman riding around on a bike these days! It would be a welcome sight but for sure he'd get knocked off!

The doctor's surgery was held in the Manor once a week, there was no NHS until 1948. Dr Hillier came from Boscastle and saw his patients in the downstairs living room. He was a one-man band who worked all day and night, seven days a week and, to cap it all, he was the dentist as well. The surgery was usually well attended and from what I remember, my mother laid on lunch for the doctor and most of the patients. After lunch he drove around the parish visiting the sick and frail before returning to Boscastle. Needless to say he was a well-loved friend and his devotion was much appreciated. I shall never forget the year when Martha was involved in a serious accident. It was in the early 1950s after a heavy dump of

snow, everything in the haven was at a standstill. The field below Tremoutha was long and steep, ideal for a sleigh run. It was great fun with several huddled together, clinging on as they hurtled down over the field at top speed. A large boulder was unseen in the deep drifts of snow and Martha took the full impact as the sledge crashed into it. Fun quickly turned into fear as she lay in the snow shocked with pain and, among other things, a complicated open fracture of the leg. The bone was exposed, the roads were impassable – and so she was lifted into a trailer. Mill Ball hill and Pentreath were steep and slippery with compacted ice and so the only solution was to hoist her up the hill on a stretcher, hopefully with an ambulance waiting at the top. There was no air ambulance in those days, as a community we all pulled together if there was an emergency. If you had a serious injury you could be in hospital for months, these days you might get sent home within a few days! Martha's leg was pinned and, together with convalescence, it was a full year before my wife completely recovered.

It wasn't long before I realised the true value of a wife. Martha was a mother to three young children, cook and bottle washer, cleaner and my essential business partner. Quite apart from regular visits to the hospital I was going to have a real struggle on my hands. By now we had to fulfil school contracts and the busy season was about to begin. It was around this time that our good neighbours Bill and Vera Bragg arrived from Hartland to farm at Ludon. While the farmhouse was

Bill & Vera Bragg starting out a new life in Crackington

start from scratch. Fortunately for me Bill was a driver who welcomed some part-time work – back then everyone helped each other out. Bill was able to drive the school round, but this meant a very early start as he milked twenty cows by hand before setting out in the morning. Vera has always been a meticulous farmer's wife who opened their house to visitors; she proved a very good friend to Martha. The Humber was a challenge to drive but Bill took it in his stride. He helped us out until he expanded the farm and took over the land at Tremoutha.

My mother and Lottie looked after our two boys Paul and Clive, but my daughter was still very young and needed more care. Lottie had a toddler of her own and the Manor would soon be full with visitors so, after much deliberation, it was decided that my young daughter should be cared for by Martha's sister in London. That was an experience she would never forget. My sister-in-law lived with her husband and son, slap bang in the centre of Bayswater, London. So it was at an early age that my daughter left the quiet country backwater of Crackington to experience the sophistication of London life. Their home

snuggled in the valley looking out towards the sea, the agricultural land posed a real challenge. They were a young married couple and, although Hartland is only a few miles up the coast, Vera felt like she had come to a foreign land! Bill was an excellent farmer and soon got stuck in. From the 1950s they opened the camping field from Easter to September. There were school camps, girl guides, scouts, hikers and backpackers all pleased to find a campsite on the coastal route. The camping was a regular feature until the 1970s when they became restricted to one summer month only. To this day the couple maintain everything in tiptop order, but they also had to work hard and

Crackington in the 1950s

was in Orme Square along the Bayswater Road, opposite the gates to Kensington Gardens and Hyde Park. It was a short walk to The Serpentine where her cousin used to float his model boats. The house at Orme Square was very large with servant's quarters in the basement; it was on the corner with a rear garden, pond and a parking bay. You wouldn't recognise it today as, like so many big houses, it has been converted into apartments. If we had the opportunity to take a break we used to head for my in-laws in London. It was a

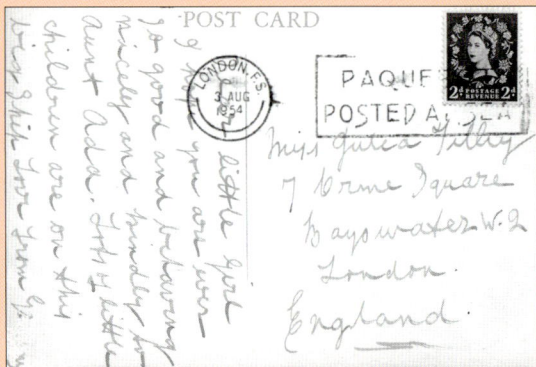

Postcard to Orme Square

long trek in years gone by, no motorways or dual carriageways and it would take all day! On one occasion we arrived late at night. With things to unpack and children to get settled into bed I was left to sort out gifts for the children. There was a riot in the morning as my eldest son discovered a doll, while my daughter had a toy car! My in-laws, Roy and Carson, were a laugh a minute and used to create some hilarious home-made games. Once he had a long table complete with model horses which were somehow wired up to race from top to bottom! Martha came from a big family so we had many relations around London

including my mother-in-law in Twickenham. They were all very hospitable and we had some wonderful times. When you stop to think about it, it was an ideal exchange for all concerned, from the coast and countryside holiday to the break in the metropolis of London! The excitement was reciprocal, when the Londoners came to visit us they had the full farm and country experience. My mother-in-law got along famously with my mother and smothered everything with a thick layer of her delicious clotted cream – even floating it on her tea! There was no shortage of children, my nephew was an only child living in Bayswater and he loved to stay with us. The pavements and parks surrounding his home were very smooth, manicured and level, which may explain why he was so accident-prone when he came to visit. My children were always keen to introduce him to all their countryside antics and invariably he would be stuck in the mud or up a tree! The bridge across the stream in the orchard had wooden planks across, it was in regular use and should have posed no threat to the youngsters but somehow Carson, being skinny, managed to slip and wedge himself between the slats! He was there for quite a while before help arrived and he was finally released.

We didn't get many breaks in London, as we were so busy. I was often out all day with the coach while Martha held the fort, serving petrol and running the beach shop. As the children grew they were roped in to help and, by the time they left school, they had full work experience in everything from running a home, shop,

Petrol station and beach shop in the 1960s

serving petrol, ice creams, farm work and assisting in the guest house. There were many capers as you can imagine, on one occasion my daughter was left in charge of the beach shop, she was only young and couldn't give change. In spite of all my tuition I don't think she ever mastered maths so I gave her a bucket of coins so folks could help themselves! She managed that all right, but when I left her with a blank cheque to order some stock things didn't go so well. I was out with the bus when the rep called, Martha was laid up with a slipped disc and Julia was put in charge of the shop! We knew the rep and thought he would understand our predicament but he clearly seized the opportunity to offload some of his less popular goods. My daughter being young should have had a good insight into the kind of things children like, but when the

stock arrived we had a few buckets, spades, kites and a very large consignment of blow-up green rabbits! Strangely enough they all sold and that year everyone went to the beach clutching an inflatable rabbit! I had to make a stool for Julia because she couldn't reach the ice cream in the freezer and it was the same story when she served petrol! Thankfully when petrol was half a crown a gallon she could persuade everyone to have four gallons, a ten-shilling note required no change, which made for easy reckoning. My daughter was a practical person who never did get her head around figures.

By the time each child had reached 17-years-old I taught them all to drive and they all did a stint of local taxi work – history repeating itself! We thought it was the right thing to send them away for some training and learn to stand on their own two feet. Paul served an apprenticeship with Rolls Royce, Clive worked in the Treasury at Whitehall and Julia spent some time training in Mayfair. Their roots were in the country, however, and they soon returned. My daughter failed miserably at maths yet, she of all people, ended up working in a bank! The boys joined me as professional drivers in the business and they all live nearby.

My eldest son Paul married a Derbyshire girl whom he met whilst working at Rolls Royce. They successfully expanded the coaching business and their son Steve is now in the drivers seat and builds his own cars. Clive married a Cornish/Italian girl from St Blazey and it was their grandson, Benjamin Tilley that featured in the *Doc Martin* series as the newborn baby born to Louisa and Martin, in a pub on Bodmin Moor. My daughter married at home here in Crackington. We should have realised what was in store when we first met my son-in-law. He came to tea and Martha really pushed the boat out. She laid up the table with the best lace tablecloth and bone china tea set, all in preparation for my daughter to introduce her boyfriend. You never know what's going to come through the door, but first impressions were of a very smart likeable young man who appeared to be a very suitable match. After an enthusiastic handshake he pronounced he could perform a trick. We watched in horror as he grabbed the corner of the tablecloth and yanked it with all his might! The entire spread ended up on the floor with all the best bone china smashed to pieces. That was our introduction to him! He was

very apologetic and explained that it usually worked, but since our bone china had a rough base it had failed to slip on the cloth! They eventually married and what an escapade that proved to be! Following tradition the wedding was held in Crackington and we opted for a marquee on the lawn at Manor Cottage. It looked wonderful draped in ribbons and swirls. Tables were set with damask cloths and a profusion of flowers and floral decorations sat waiting to be arranged. Guests were arriving from London and anticipation was building for a happy event. A wedding beside the sea in a beautiful location is everyone's dream, but we awoke in the early hours of the morning to discover a nightmare! A freak gale had blown in from the sea overnight and gusts of up to 40 miles per hour had blown the marquee over! The large poles dressed in ribbons had collapsed and managed to flatten most of the tables, not a single flower remaining intact. While my carefully tended lawn was now squidgy with large portions of turf gouged out, the wind had now abated and the sun was out. Panic now ensued! After a debate over the magnitude of the gale the company finally agreed to re-erect the marquee, this time anchoring it with substantial and unsightly ropes to a tree in the river. Martha was in a flap as guests were running around like headless chickens, some with wheelbarrows of turf and others fixing tables. The caterers arrived, threw their hands in the air and declared it a disaster zone; they couldn't possibly function in a kitchen filled with cleaners.

Family weddings

It was mayhem and pandemonium, but too late to change the venue. Most brides spend the morning preening themselves, but my daughter was up to her eyes in the clean up. She was marrying a hairdresser and was probably the only bride ever who had scraped her hair back under the veil and hoped for the best!

Our good neighbours Bill and Vera came to the rescue once again and Vera's mother took over in the kitchen to help save the day!

The in-laws arrived all calm and toffed off but I always said if my son-in-law fell down a sewer he would come up with his hair parted! Barring a few headless

flowers the event turned out all right. The only hitch involved the photographer who chose to launch himself on to one of the broken tables put aside and covered in cloth. Having got himself a champion view of the proceedings he didn't realise he was in considerable danger as the table swayed from side to side. The subsequent photographs portrayed guests displaying a mixture of restrained laughter and uneasy disquiet. No videos back then, but someone had a new fangled cine camera and kindly filmed guests coming and going through the door at Manor Cottage. Unfortunately it was not the main door to the house, but the outside loo! So we have a memorable film of all those guests adjusting their best attire as they departed from the little room.

Colour television had just come onto the market and a new communal mast

TILLEY'S MARSHGATE-BUDE SERVICE FRIDAYS ONLY			
MARSHGATE	9.30	BUDE STRAND	12.30
TRESPARRETT	9.32	MARHAMCHURCH	12.40
TRESPARRETT POST	9.35	HELEBRIDGE	12.45
HIGHER CRACKINGTON	9.40	DIMMA CHAPEL	13.00
CRACKINGTON HAVEN	9.45	JACOBSTOW	13.05
WHITE LODGE	9.50	WAINHOUSE CORNER	13.10
WAINHOUSE CORNER	9.55	WHITE LODGE	13.15
JACOBSTOW	10.00	CRACKINGTON HAVEN	13.20
DIMMA CHAPEL	10.05	HIGHER CRACKINGTON	13.25
HELEBRIDGE	10.15	TRESPARRETT POST	13.30
MARHAMCHURCH	10.20	TRESPARRETT	13.33
BUDE STRAND	10.30	MARSHGATE	13.35

Bus service timetable

had been erected on Penkenna. A real novelty so all the male guests crowded into the lounge to watch the cup final in glorious technicolour, while all the youngsters took off to the beach! My mother was serene and undisturbed, no doubt reflecting on her own wedding day in Crackington sixty-two years ago to the day. She was probably wondering what on earth the world was coming to!

The Dearloves wedding reception at the Manor

In the Driving Seat

Clive in front of the Humber Pullman

During the war petrol was not available for private use. There was a restriction of about a 10-mile radius for essential or work purposes. Larger vehicles were taken and converted into vans or ambulances for the war effort, any vehicle not absolutely necessary had to be immobilised. Even after the war there were tight restrictions, economies had been devastated and it was a very difficult time of strikes and unrest. I had assisted in the Longbridge factory during wartime, while stationed at Leamington Spa. The place was buzzing with activity and there were some excellent workers there. Soon after the war the factory returned to car production but it wasn't long before gangs of good workers were out on strike. It was a hard time for everyone, we had all endured World War 2 thinking it would restore freedom and give us a better chance in life. It was 1950 before the petrol rationing finally stopped, there were very few vehicles around then, but it wouldn't be long before people would turn to motoring. Everyone was weary of rations and restrictions and began to think about rebuilding their lives. It was the beginning of holidays and travel.

My time in the army had given me training in mechanical engineering and a lot of experience in driving, it had influenced the path I would take. After the war I bought a variety of cars to use as taxis. The first was a Standard 9hp and then the more powerful Hillman 21hp. They were a far cry from cars today and made for some hair-raising driving with the hills we have around here! A job to imagine it now but gradually some locals were getting mobile. Tom Sandercock was driving around in his Morris Cowley with a dickie seat and the Jose family at Churchtown had a Morris Saloon. Mr Stacey retired, built Boskenna and then he bought an Austin 12.

It was the Hillman that had a leaky roof, I tried everything I could think of to seal the leak. You have to understand that there was no such thing as sealer or duct tape so it was a challenge to seal the stitched seams in the hood. I always hoped it would be fine weather if a taxi was required, but typically one day when it was lashing down with rain, I was called

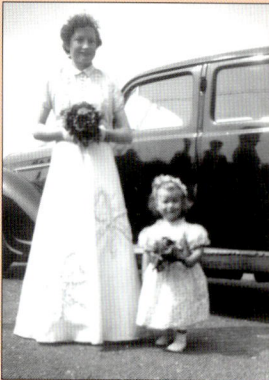

The wedding car in the early 1950s

Humber Pullman Mascot.

to take an elderly lady to Launceston. All went well for the first few miles and I thought I had solved the problem, then I glanced in the mirror and there she was sat bolt upright with her umbrella up to keep her hair dry! She was a real lady, a gentle person who appreciated everything you did and never complained. Not everyone was so easy, we had one man who hired me to take him to the top of Boscastle to collect potatoes and onions. From the top it was a ride across some fields to the potato and onion patch and, once there, I could hardly sit and watch him dig them up by himself! It was a time consuming job and we'd end up smothered in mud with a boot load of spuds! Driving back through Boscastle he would ask to stop for a minute, he would leap out of the car and into The Cobweb, the local pub. After an hour or two I would look in to see if he was ready to go home, but no chance. There he would be larking about playing darts and drinking beer!

The Humber Pullman was a grand car, it was a smart 7-seater with a wind up privacy screen, deep plush carpet and a cocktail cabinet in the back. It was a heavily built substantial car, which few people could drive. On the bonnet was a Pegasus horse mascot with wings. Best known in Greek mythology as a divine stallion, they were fixed on to Humber Pullmans in 1936. Divine or not I couldn't stand the thing! It was weird and protruded out front, so I was in constant risk of clouting myself on it and afraid it would give me a poke in the eye! On the plus side it was very useful for securing wedding ribbons and really looked the part. The Humber was smart in polished black, ideal for special occasions, in much demand for weddings and I felt like a real chauffeur when I drove it.

Early Days of Tilley's Tours

I purchased my first bus in 1951, there had been no buses manufactured during the war years so it was an older 1930s style Bedford. I constantly adjusted the brakes but you never quite knew how they would respond. Hot made them sluggish, or cold made them fierce enough to put you through the windscreen! It didn't

I didn't think twice about it then but now, when I look back, I wonder how on earth I managed it!

It helped being familiar with the area of course and all its snags and pitfalls. One hill that really gave me the heebie-jeebies was at Dunmere, where there was a level crossing. No safety barriers then and I was always pleased to get to the other side in case a train was coming and the brakes got hot!

I took a fully booked coachload on a day trip to see the lovely area of Lynton and Lynmouth. In those days there was a

Chauffeur to William Pridham and his bride Dorothy Northcott

...and Gordon and Jean Teague

matter where you went with the bus it would be steep and narrow. The school run around the parish started with a long, slow pull out of the haven and then in and out of all the lanes and eventually down into Churchtown. I used to drive the bus out beyond Dizzard on the top of the Millook Road; I doubt whether anyone else has driven a bus over there! It is without doubt a very narrow road and, to this day, it isn't even possible to drive a bus through Millook itself. I had to turn around in a tight lane at the top of the hill.

large tank of water halfway up Lynton Hill, intended to cool boiling radiators and an escape road that you could slip into if your brakes failed. A good idea, because you could steer a runaway vehicle into a gravel slip road and the wheels would gradually sink until the vehicle stops. Lynton is about 600ft above Lynmouth and the hill in those days was a challenging gradient. There was a gorge below and for good reason the area was known as Little Switzerland. Well, we were steadily ascending the steep gradient

55581. Crackington Haven.

without any problem at all, that was until a passenger reached out and grabbed my seat and unexpectedly yanked me backwards! As we reached a critically high viewpoint on the hill Granny Ambrose, being on the small side, wanted to hoist herself up to get a better view out of the window. The drivers' seats in those days were adjustable, not like today's adjustable seats that are firmly fixed with lever controls. No, back then seats would tilt forward and back. I had taken the precaution of fixing the seat forward before setting off up the hill, but a forceful yank from behind was all that was required to tilt the seat backwards. The hill up towards Lynton is notoriously steep and the driver, apart from concentrating, needed to be sat as far forward as possible to reach the pedals and see through the windscreen. While Granny Ambrose enjoyed a spectacular view of the precarious drop over the hillside into the gorge below, I was left clinging on to the wheel, neck stretched and forcing myself forward – every muscle in my body wrenched to keep my foot on the pedal! These days passengers are strapped in with safety belts, and while coach windows offer better views the driver has full control over his seat. As for Granny Ambrose, she was affectionately known as Granny to all because she was a sweet, harmless little lady who was very small and wore granny glasses. She thoroughly enjoyed her days out and managed to get a good view out of the window. She would have been most upset had she known the consequences of her actions, but there was no need as we all arrived

safe and sound. There have been great strides in engineering and vast improvements over the years, as all vehicles have become much safer. I am pleased to say that I never came to grief. In time I had coaches that were so smooth I could drive with a saucer of water on the bonnet without a spill! The Ministry of Transport set up stringent inspections and I always had a good relationship with them. Coaches now are the complete opposite to those early days, comfortable, very easy to drive with all the latest technology, power steering, excellent braking and all mod cons.

Years ago the bus was kept around the back of Manor Cottage near the meadow. One morning I set off up the hill as usual and the first pickup was about a mile or so at Middle Crackington. I had just pulled over when I was rather shocked! I recognised our chickens crossing the road in front of me, quite unperturbed. There must have been about a dozen bantam hens strutting out in a line. They had roosted overnight on the rear axle and had been rudely awakened by the ride! None the worse for their adventure they were now being adopted by a family on top of the hill, so I could continue my journey.

The day I took the Women's Institute to St Mawes we nearly missed the ferry back. It wasn't unusual to have to wait a few minutes for someone, but I was anxious as we had to catch the King Harry ferry and we were delayed. It's a very narrow lane as we approached the river and I could see the last ferry was already halfway across to the other side. That caused some excitement as there was absolutely no way

The Saltash ferry pulls away from the Cornish bank on its ceremonial crossing of the Tamar yesterday to mark the end of the 600-year-old service.

The Saltash Ferry in 1961

of turning the bus around to go back. Thankfully the ferryman saw our plight and returned for us, just as well or I would have had to spend the night with a busload of excitable women on the slipway! In the early 1950s the King Harry functioned with chains powered by steam. The crossing is known to be one of the most picturesque and these days it is powered by other means. It is exceptionally scenic along the River Fal. There used to be a steam powered ferry across the Tamar, it was known as the

floating bridge and was replaced by the new Tamar Bridge. There was quite a celebration when the last ferry departed and opening the Tamar Bridge was a significant change. Another unexpected event happened on one of my excursions to Plymouth when I came across an accident. A car had collided with a motorbike, the rider lay injured while his bike was on fire. It was a trifle embarrassing to see the news headlines the next day with a very unfortunate photograph excluding the extinguisher!

Bus tours around Cornwall were very much in demand. I travelled all over the county and those were happy times. It is a beautiful area and there was no better way to see the scenery, with clear views over the hedges. We visited all the beauty spots, fishing villages, gardens, plus shopping trips and theatre outings. On one of the day trips to Looe, I had my young daughter on board. It was a calm, sunny day so I decided to take my daughter out on a fishing trip. I had cast the line in the hope of catching some mackerel and we sat and waited patiently. Suddenly we noticed a tug on the line and excitedly began to wind the reel in to reveal the catch. The next thing we knew the boat was being heaved up into the air from the underside. We looked overboard and were shocked to see a massive shark! We had caught a shark! It was circling around us under the boat, nudging us from underneath and trying to tip us up! We were absolutely terrified and have never been fishing since.

Pantomime was popular in winter and then there were the shows at Plymouth. In

Using an extinguisher from a passing coach which he was driving, Mr. A. T. Tilley, of Manor Garage, Crackington Haven, puts out a fire which practically destroyed a motorcycle in Tavistock-road, Plymouth, today. The motor-cycle, ridden by Mr. Kiernan Mallaghan, of 19, Woolwich-cottages, Crownhill, burst into flames after a collision with a car. Mr. Tilley's coach was first in a long line of traffic held up by the blazing obstruction. He leapt from his cab, and, with the extinguisher, had the fire out in a few minutes. Mr. Mallaghan had burns injured and also obtained a fractured wrist. He was taken by ambulance to Freedom Fields Hospital.

RAID ON G.P.O. FOILED

Caught extinguishing the fire

the 1960s my youngest children were entering their teens just when the pop scene began. Plymouth Theatre sent out advertisements for the pop concerts and my youngsters would jump up and down with excitement. I would have given it a miss, but Clive and Julia soon rallied around enough to fill the bus and off we went to see every pop concert that performed in Plymouth in the 60s. Well, practically every band, singer and group came to Plymouth Theatre. Cilla Black, The Shadows, Dusty Springfield, Sandie Shaw, The Searchers, Roy Orbison, The Dave Clark Five, The Kinks and so it went on. Then one day, during their first tour, we were offered tickets for The Beatles! My son had a black Beatles jacket and my daughter had the full regalia, all black Beatles clothes and even Beatles stockings! They were eager and the bus was full, but one sad teenager was strictly forbidden to attend any pop concerts. She was, however, absolutely determined to go and see the Beatles. Her parents were older and put great importance on her piano tuition and classical music. Having been through the lectures about the unsuitable and undesirable content of these pop concerts the girl, in her desperate plight, exclaimed to her father that the Beatles would be playing an excerpt from Mozart. Or maybe it was Roll Over Beethoven! Whatever it was it did the trick and she was one very excited teenager on board the bus that night! My daughter had strict instructions, to sit quietly with her brother and no screaming. My son lost control as soon as the Fab Four arrived on stage. When I looked in, my daughter was

jumping up and down and screaming her head off! You couldn't hear a thing! Travelling home in the bus the youngsters were excitable, singing and clinging to their programmes, posters and photographs. The wall in my daughter's bedroom was plastered in big black and white Beatles' posters. There were some good times back then.

Most of the roads around the parish are single track with no central white lines, so it's expected that you ease up or pull over if you meet oncoming traffic. Not so for

Generation game: Three generations of the Tilley family are working together to weather the recession.

many! I had been in the driver's seat since I was seventeen but had to surrender my licence when my sight began to fail. I had been driving just about every day for over 80 years and found it very hard to become a passenger, especially as most of my friends had become older and a touch doddery. One friend used to take me to play bowls, he was a good chap and it was kind of him but, like so many, he drove down the centre of the road oblivious to oncoming cars. The roads around the parish have become busy these days, many times we would meet someone in a narrow spot or on a bend. With their fists clenched, mad at him, they would wave their arms in the air! My friend would wave back happily and say, "There's someone else who knows us Alf!" Maybe it's me? My daughter has been driving for nearly 50 years and she tells me I am still giving her lessons! On the plus side she says she doesn't need a sat nav when I'm sat beside her. Anyway you don't need to sit at home and mope because there are some very good mobility scooters on the market, I charge mine up and get out most days. It's surprising just how far you can go and I can explore many places off the beaten track you just can't reach with a car. I'm sorry I can't take passengers any more!

Tilley's Coaches

COACH TOURS	PRIVATE HIRE	TAXI SERVICE
"MANOR GARAGE"		Telephone:
CRACKINGTON HAVEN		ST. GENNYS
CORNWALL		244

1960s in the Haven

Three Halls and a Judge

The first institute was a railway carriage that had been converted into a social club; Squire Harris donated it for the men of St Gennys. As a young lad I had to conform to the club rules if I wanted to join in the games, which were darts, bagatelle and a ring board. Harry Rogers from Hallagather was a member and Charlie Cobbledick was the caretaker. By the 1950s the old club was to be replaced by a new village hall, where women could join in the activities. It took over five years to raise £2,000; there were all kinds of fundraising activities and volunteers to help dig the foundations as there were no grants in those days. Uncle Frank Ward donated the land and everyone had put in a tremendous effort before the institute

Judge Scobell-Armstrong & Julia at the Institute opening in May 1955

The Luncheon

was finally opened in May 1955. Thomas Teague presented the keys, Judge Scobell-Armstrong gave the opening speech, my daughter gave him a boutonnière and my father, as the institute president, gave a vote of thanks. Over the years the hall has been the hub of many social occasions and

A delightful touch was the presentation to his Honour of a boutonniere by little Julia Tilley, granddaughter of the Institute's president. For the 78-year-old judge, who is proud to describe himself as a Victorian, turned with old-world courtesy to lift the little girl's hand to his lips and kiss it. Then Julia, with all the unconscious dignity of her four years, responded with an equally stately curtsey.

The ladies of the parish showed the reason for their high reputation as organisers by the nature of the spread they provided at the luncheon which followed. The Mayor of Launceston (Coun. C. H. Robins) presided, in his first official appearance since his election as chief citizen of the borough the previous day. Speakers were Mr. Alan Parnall, J.P., Miss M. I. M. Douglass, Judge Scobell Armstrong, Coun. W. Boney, C.C., Rev. A. L. Parish (Vicar of St. Gennys), Mr. C. Bloomer (Parish Clerk), and Mrs. Audrey Snook.

A comprehensive vote of thanks was given to everyone concerned by the Institute President (Mr. W. T. Tilley).

THE HELPERS.

The floral decorations for the day were done by Mr. and Mrs. Richie. Helpers at the luncheon were Mesdames C. Chapman, H. Biscombe, S. Botterall, J. Ward, R. Teague, jnr., H. Stuttaford, L. Ward, A. Wright, F. Ward, T. Ward, R. Pooley, M. Teague, W. Edwards, W. Marshall, F. Bird, J. Biscombe, M. Bird, E. Rogers, C. J. Sandercock, A. Tilley and Misses D. Rogers, B. Rogers, G. Heal, R. Pickard, N. Crowle and Master Michael Sandercock. The door steward was Mr. L. Ward. Dainty buttonholes were made and sold by Miss Maureen Stuttaford.

The secretary of the Women's Section of the Institute (Mrs. E. Sandercock) was responsible for the luncheon and tea, and all the Women's Committee worked hard.

The interior and exterior decorations were carried out by Messrs. C. J. and M. Sandercock.

A field was lent for a car park by Mr. R. Rogers.

A sale of work and various other stalls were declared open by Mrs. West Stephens, of Rugby, who was then presented with a bouquet by four-years-old Rex Ward (grandson of Mr. and Mrs. F. Ward, the donors of the building site). The various stallholders and assistants were: Mesdames W. Piper, F. Tape, R. Rogers, G. Heal, E. F. Gliddon, H. Teague and Mrs. Bunney.

During the afternoon selections were rendered by St. Gennys Silver Band, conducted by their Deputy Bandmaster (Mr. F. Knight).

Proceedings were enlivened by a number of popular sideshows in charge of the following: Cricket ball, treasure hunt, Mrs. Richie; skittles, E. L. Gliddon and J. Tape; hoop-la, Mrs. R. Teague, senr., Miss J. Cowling and Roger Teague; pennies-in-bath, Mr. H. Stuttaford; dart board, Mr. A. Hancock; lucky wheel, Mr. Olde; guessing weight of sheep, Mr. G. Smith. Tea was served by the gentlemen (assisted by some ladies):— Messrs. W. Crowle, C. J. Sandercock, W. J. Pickard, W. J. Sandercock, M. Teague, R. Polatch, J. Ward, N. Teague, T. Teague, W. G. Gliddon, A. Tilley, E. Rogers, M. Sandercock, S. Botterall, E. F. Gliddon and F. Tape.

At an auction sale, the auctioneer was Mr. Peter Kivell, who was introduced by Mr. W. Piper. All the articles for the sale were collected by Messrs. W. Piper and R. B. Sandercock.

A friendly football match was played between a Wainhouse Corner team and a Crackington team. The referee was Mr. H. Brown, and the linesmen were Messrs. B. Ward and A. Medland. The match resulted in a draw, 1-1.

In the evening a grand concert was given by the Mid-Cornwall Prize Male Quartette, assisted by Mr. John Elford (elocutionist) and Mr. David Bazeley (trombone soloist). The accompanist was Mrs. A. Mills. Mr. J. H. Parsons (Halworthy) took the chair, and the artistes were introduced by Mr. W. Crowle, who also announced the winners of the various sideshows: Treasure hunt, Mr. Greenaway (Wilsea); skittles, Mr. A. Bright; darts, Mr. D. Rogers; weight of sheep (correct weight 118lbs.), Mr. D. Ward-Pinkney (120lbs.). No one guessed the name (Sophia) of a doll (given and dressed by Miss Neal, of Camelford, and in charge of Miss N. Crowle) but the doll was won in a further competition by Mrs. M. Teague. The number of peas in the jar was 2,555, and the prize, a tray of sweets, chocolate and fruit, given by Mrs. R. Rogers, was won by Mr. Edgar Ward.

A vote of thanks was given by Mr. Crowle and Mr. Parsons suitably replied.

Originally the gift of the late Squire Harris, then owner of the Manor of Crackington, the old Institute building has not yet ended its long life of usefulness. One suggestion was that it should be preserved alongside the new Hall as an example to future generations of what had been achieved by the present generation, but, in fact, it has been sold, and will shortly take up a new role: that of a chicken house.

There to watch the opening of its successor was Mr. H. J. Rogers (Hallagather), now over 80, the only surviving member of the Institute when first opened.

ST. GENNYS CRACKINGTON INSTITUTE.

OPENING OF NEW HALL

Tuesday, May 24th, 1955.

LUNCHEON

TICKETS 5/-

Above: Luncheon ticket

Left: Newsclip 1955

now, some sixty years later, it has been completely overhauled into yet another new hall with sports facilities. I have enjoyed social activities in all three institutes. Henry Hall, the big band player used to spend a lot of time in Crackington and he gave us a prized cup for the darts competition. My father left a cup for snooker and he would have enjoyed the instruction and demonstration given by Ray Reardon when he opened the new snooker club.

The Post Office and General Store is now situated at Higher Crackington, opposite the village hall. Originally the general store was a carpenter's shop where they used to make cartwheels of wood with metal rims, but now it's popular with the new community built in the 1970s. A new housing estate was built at Brockhill, for the first time there were pavements and street lights introduced into the parish. This was urbanisation and without a doubt one of the biggest changes in this area for decades.

As for the Honourable Judge Scobell-Armstrong he was nearly 80-years-old when he opened the new village hall. He was a perfectly dignified gentleman who earned a lot of respect. During his time he'd made a brilliant judge, as he appeared to have the Wisdom of Solomon! We could do with justice like that today. I recall one case which he took very seriously. Animals can get very attached to their owners and, as I remember, two neighbouring farmers had a real ding-dong over a cow! It was back in the 1940s when both farmers were claiming it to be their own. The farms were at Boscastle and Fred Jewell worked as herdsman caring for cattle on one of these. The dispute became so serious that it ended up going to Camelford County Court where Judge Scobell-Armstrong handled the case. After sitting for hours listening to testimonies from either side, the judge used his wisdom and took the matter to the field. Both farmers were asked to gather their cows and herdsman on either side of the field, the disputed cow was then led out to the middle for an identity parade! It immediately recognised Fred Jewell as his herdsman, nudging her nose affectionately up Fred's back then jumping up as if to claim her owner and end the

Alfred & Martha with the first village hall in the background

dispute. Fred used to encourage the cows to jump up from behind him and he would hold onto them with their hooves around his waist. Judge Scobell-Armstrong was highly impressed and certain that this was conclusive evidence, completing proceedings by saying that the cow had been reunited with the man who had won her affection! This all happened over 70 years ago but I have never forgotten it. I can't imagine a judge doing that today. Justice is another thing that's gone topsy-turvy!

Handing over the keys

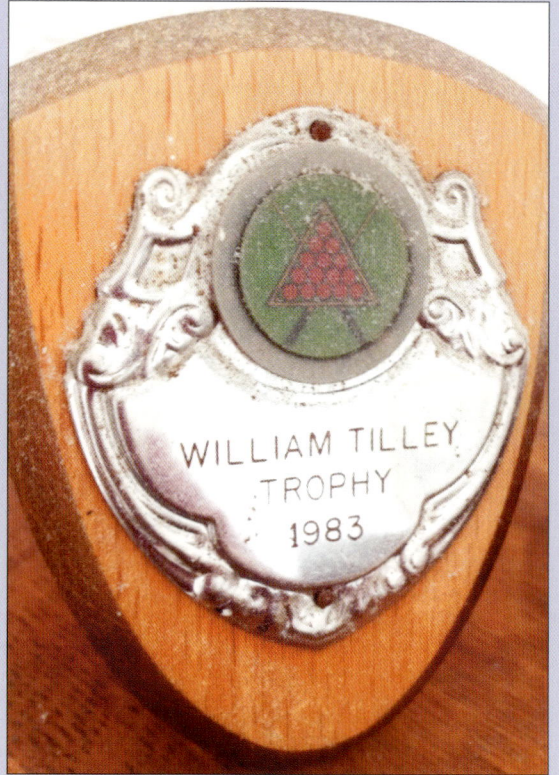

William Tilley trophy

Snooker club

Carnival

With Ray Reardon

Coast

Approached by steep winding narrow roads, Crackington Haven is off the beaten track and split into two halves with the river creating the north and south divide. St Gennys is a rural area with farms and smallholdings throughout the parish, as agriculture has always been the main livelihood. Like so many Cornish coves the hills and cliffs either side of the valley are dramatic. Heather, gorse and bracken create a rich tapestry across the skyline with the sea far below. The cliffs are stunning and, on the north side of the beach, Penkenna is the dominant one. It rises four hundred feet above the ocean. We have always known it as Penkenna, a hill with pastures on the top, but the maps sometimes show Pencannow Point, which

Millook

I believe refers to the rocky crag at the point. Either way it is a magnificent stretch of headland with far-reaching coastal views. These days there is the recognised long distance South West Coast Path that enables you to walk over the heather-clad cliffs and through valleys of steep wooded ravines, where the light is dappled and you may welcome the shade. From Somerset to Dorset, it's a full 630 miles if you feel so inclined! The path between Crackington and Bude is strenuous but spectacular and much the same as I have ever known it. From Penkenna the path leads across the Barton fields to Churchtown and the old school; venturing on you will eventually come to the Butterfly Valley beyond Dizzard. Trees along this coast have little chance of growing upright, they are all stunted and turn inland. Here you will find ancient oaks in a bonsai forest before you reach Millook. The zigzag patterns in the rock face have drawn folks from all over the world – it is fascinating to see how the earth has been forced up into folds. Surrounded in nature the wildlife was more prolific when I was younger. At night there would be many owls, not just

one or two. Glow-worms were another creature I remember, dozens of them glimmering in the dark. Scores of butterflies were present of every variety and there were many more birds. In the autumn the sky would go dark with the displays of thousands of starlings swooping across the sky. Swallows returned year after year to the same nesting spot to raise their young. I remember the dawn chorus from years gone by, something you never forget. Recently I told a friend about it and we decided to relive the experience, so one

Sketch showing the South West Coast Path

morning we emerged before dawn and entered the woods to listen. We waited patiently expecting an orchestral delight of chirps and trills, but there was silence! Not a single song to be heard. And I may be old but I'm not deaf! The sun rose and we eventually made our way home where a few birds were happily singing and chirping away in the garden.

We were southerners. The south side cliff path is much easier with equally breathtaking scenery as you ascend above Tremoutha Haven. There are some good circular walks if you continue up to Woodgate and down through East Wood, well known post routes. The coastal path takes you up to the Cams, Strangles and High Cliff, the latter being the highest sea cliff in Cornwall at over seven hundred feet above sea level. The next village is tucked away along the coast at Boscastle. This is where you see the quaint Cornish cottages along the harbour and through the old village. It is surprising to see a harbour here as it is as rugged and treacherous as you can imagine, which just goes to show how desperate the villagers were to trade years ago. Everything heavy was transported by sea. To see the best of the coast and village you need to climb the path beyond the harbour, up towards the old coastal lookout tower, then up to the top of the village. You will pass the Forrabury Stitches, which is an example of medieval style farming. It must have been a struggle to get anything to grow on those strips of land, being open and exposed to the south westerly gales and salt-laden air. There are wonderful views from here before finding your way back down to the harbour through the quaint old village.

Tourism has become the main industry today; easy access to the coast and a mild climate draws people to these far-flung areas. In the past the Cornish have had to rely on the land and sea around them for survival – and it was tough. Ships sailing from Lands End towards Bristol often met with stormy seas and heavy gales, every year dozens of vessels floundered and were wrecked along the coast. Folks relied on imported goods such as lime, coal and timber. Locally-produced goods such as slate, potatoes and minerals were exported. My parents spoke about the limekiln, which was located on the south side of the beach. It was filled with layers of lime and coal which, after a burning

Remains of the kiln

process, was used to reduce the acidity of the soil. The kiln disappeared gradually with the erosion of the cliff. Slate was quarried from the rocks in Crackington and used in local building and for export. It was all labour-intensive work, exceptionally dangerous; men fell from the cliffs and lost their lives as they struggled to lift the heavy slabs. Loads were transported over the cliffs at Penkenna, Tremoutha and Strangles by donkeys or packhorse. My ancestors lived in Crackington at the time and would have had first-hand experience of what it was like. Thankfully I wasn't around then! There have been various accounts written over the years and history varies. All I know is there were no tourists at the time, no picnics and no one stretched out on the beach enjoying the sun. It was a question of working to survive. During my lifetime I remember sand being dredged and loaded near Harlyn Bay by Padstow. In Crackington I recall the large amounts of stone being crushed on the north side of the beach, many heaps piled up high and used by the Rural District Council for road building around the parish. This went on for months. The north side of the beach was privately owned by different individuals, originally leased from the Duchy. There was a slipway for folks to launch boats and a public path. The beachhead on the south side was originally all part of the Crackington Manor estate and my father sold the dam field and some adjoining land on the Tremoutha side to the Parnell family. The Duchy owned several acres of the beach and, in 1935, it was going to be sold for private use. Years before the harbour scheme had been aborted my father, now on the parish council, became aware of another scheme. He was anxious to maintain the area for public enjoyment, but St Gennys Parish Council did not have the funds to purchase the beach, so my father stepped in and bought it on their behalf. In appreciation he was given permission to collect beach material for his own use during his lifetime. When Reg Burden died he left a plot of land for the parish to use as a car park. He stipulated that income be used first for maintenance and the surplus to be distributed to St Gennys charities. In more recent times the Legion Hall was transferred by those who had served in the war to the local parish council. The Parnell family donated part of the Tremoutha cliffs to the National Trust. Years ago we used to take a wheelbarrow down and collect gravel which we subsequently used for building. That all happened a very long time ago and would never happen now. The beach constantly changes, it never stays the same. Storms and high tides determine the shape of it, drag boulders out and strip it of sand. There has been considerable erosion at the beachhead, the highest tide I have ever seen swamped the south side, a huge wave hit the cliff which must have exceeded 40ft! This unusual event had drawn spectators to the beachhead and everyone thought they were at a safe distance, but Frank Tape had to rescue aunty Jane Rogers or she would have been washed out to sea. She was stood near the sandpit wall when a freak wave suddenly rose high above us and crashed down with immense strength demolishing the wall and dragging the boulders away as it went back. I have never seen anything quite like that since. During a recent storm all the sand disappeared from Crackington, while further down the coast, roads and properties were buried under several feet of sand. Another high tide and everything changes again, sand comes and goes. As they say, tide and time waits for no man.

St Gennys Parish Council

22.8.1946

At our last Council meeting matters concerning the Foreshore came up for discussion.
The Councillors felt sure in their own minds, that it is mainly due to your efforts and generosity that the Parish now owns the Rights of the Foreshore at Crackington Haven. The Council from a sense of duty, & justice as well as appreciation passed the enclosed resolution. It is my duty and also a pleasure to pass it on to you, and I trust you will be able to enjoy the privilege for many years.

Yours faithfully,
CR Smeeth. Clerk

Resolution. Privilege to Mr W Tilley
Mr William Thomas Tilley is granted by St Gennys Parish Council permission to take free of charge from Crackington Haven Foreshore, stones shingle and sand which he may need for his personal use at Crackington Manor. This permission does not permit the taking of shingle though for the purpose of making concrete posts as a matter of business. Furthermore the privilege is granted to Mr Tilley personally & cannot be passed on to any other owners or tenants of Crackington Manor.

The Railway

In the early 1800s it was considered essential to provide a safe harbour for vessels sailing between Lands End and Ilfracombe. The plan was to extend the railway network from Launceston to Crackington and build a harbour with a lighthouse at Tremoutha Haven; the surveys and plans were drawn and it was proposed to build a new town called Victoria. Decisions were made by Parliament and an Act was passed in 1836. Trinity House gave the go-ahead for the lighthouse on Cam Beak and plans to build the railway were in motion. I can't imagine what local people must have thought about it and for certain they wouldn't have a say. It took over six years to extend the railway from Launceston to Tresmeer, the station was actually at Splatt but they obviously didn't like that name! Otterham Station finally opened in August 1893. The plan to extend to Crackington and the new town of Victoria was abandoned because, amongst other things, it was taking too long. The company found it difficult obtaining the land, although much would have been by compulsory purchase. The main town was planned to extend from Knap beyond the top of Mill Ball, right down into the valley on the south side, then part of the original Crackington Manor Estate. Approximately 40 houses were to be built on a very steep incline with a new road in the middle. In the valley a large development was planned from Grey Roofs through towards Congdons with a roundabout at the end. Another 30 houses were planned on the north side of Crackington, below Lovers

Walk towards the east and Lovers Lane at the west end. There must have been a big sigh of relief and much delight in the village when the plans for a town were aborted. Some individual sites have been developed much later, Coombe Gate was site 37, Seacroft was site 34 and the Nook site 16. The station up the road at Otterham was ideally situated and welcomed. Plans to extend the railway line to Truro were also abandoned but the line to Padstow was much easier, other than the Petherick Bridge. It was finally completed in 1912. Today there are many harbours along the coast. Padstow and

Bude linked with the railway and enabled fishermen to send their catch to distant markets. The railway changed everything. Goods arrived and departed from the station and there were trucks to carry cattle to markets. The railway also signalled the real beginning of the holiday trade as visitors could finally access the West Country by train. Newquay was one of the first notable holiday resorts in Cornwall, with places like Crackington relatively undiscovered, until more recently.

My great grandparents were living locally when the railway and harbour plans were proposed; they were relying on the Royal Mail Coaching Service then. My grandparents lived through the Victorian era and my parents were present when the railway station opened at Otterham. There were celebrations when the first trains arrived, but my mother was still alive when Mr Beeching closed the railway. The last train was packed and everyone knew it was a bad decision – there were no celebrations then! All very sad because now roads are congested with lorries and juggernauts trying to deliver goods countrywide; everyone is concerned about pollution. Wrecks along the coast have been replaced by wrecks on roads; you take your life in your hand once you drive down some of our country lanes! It's all clear along the disused railway lines though. You can cycle along unhindered, the most popular being from Wadebridge to Padstow with some lovely scenery.

The beach at Tremoutha and Crackington remain unspoilt and the haven escaped major development. Bude and Padstow have become very popular with tourists who will find plenty of restaurants in these coastal resorts. There are also good walks, cycle paths and a wonderful canal towpath at Bude. I wonder what our ancestors would make of the changes. They had hard lives and risked harvest failure and famine. There was little else to support them in times of need, a stark contrast to today as everything is geared towards leisure, burger bars and gourmet restaurants. Sometimes it is good to stop and look back to help us appreciate what we have today.

Surf Life Saving Club

The hut on the south side has served as a surf club for many decades. Originally a wooden chalet, it was then replaced by a stone building organised by Roger Teague and pals. My cousin, Leonard Ward, was a keen surfer and one of the first to use a Malibu board. In the early years the club had surf skis, wooden boards that you sat on and paddled to catch a wave. At the beachhead there was a siren and emergency line, which the group regularly used to practice running down to the sea to haul someone in. It was all voluntary back then and a case of whoever happened to be on hand. The surf club members were an enthusiastic bunch who learnt all the techniques of resuscitation and so forth. They entered life-saving competitions and they were very good. As my daughter sat on the cliff watching the practice sessions she was eager to join in, but it was strictly a men's club and no females allowed! Very often the first thing visitors want to do on arrival is go for a dip in the sea and, sometimes, regardless of the tidal conditions. It was frustrating for the team to learn that some visitors had been caught in a current and dragged out to sea and the only couple to hear the screams for help were complete novices. My daughter had watched the technique many times and so she instinctively grabbed the line and headed down the beach, while another man bravely volunteered to swim out. He was not a strong swimmer but was prepared to risk his life on behalf of a stranger. With turbulent seas and strong currents it was an anxious time, but they managed to haul

Newspaper cuttings and the Surf Life Saving Club jumper

'NO-NAME' MAN BRINGS SWIMMER ASHORE

Two women pull another in

TWO young men—holiday visitors from Middlesex—who got into difficulties while swimming in heavy surf at high tide at Crackington Haven yesterday, shouted for help as they were swept out on a rip current, but only a few people were on the beach at the time.

One of the young men, David Faulkner, of Feltham, was brought ashore by another visitor, aged about 20, who refused to give his name, and though not a strong swimmer went out on the end of a rescue line, held by 17-year-old Julia Tilley, of the Manor Garage, Crackington.

The other man, Kenneth Norris of Ashford, was swept across the cove towards some rocks on the southern side and was pulled ashore by his wife and Mrs. Faulkner, who waded out towards him through the breakers.

Mr. Philip Freestone, of the nearby Coombe Barton Hotel, ran to the beach with a malibu-board on hearing the klaxon warning being sounded, but on his arrival the men had been brought to safety.

No panic

Mr. Freestone, a surf club member, commented later: "There was no panic, which probably prevented a fatality. The wives kept their heads admirably in the emergency. The surf club is much obliged to the anonymous visitor and to Miss Tilley for their courageous and efficient action."

The bathers were first taken to Penkenna House, near the foreshore, where Mrs. R. J. Burden rang for an ambulance, which arrived from Bude 20 minutes later.

SURF LIFE SAVING EXAMINATIONS.

SUCCESSES AT BUDE AND AT CRACKINGTON HAVEN.

A team of eight members of Bude police took the bronze medallion examination of the British Surf Life Saving Association at Crooklets Beach on Sunday—and all were successful. This was a particularly fine achievement in view of the fact that the team was formed only in the early summer of this year. Members had put in hours of hard training on land and in the water to reach the necessary high standard of proficiency. The successful candidates were Det.-Cons. Wilson, Police Constables Boyling, Matthews, Pedlar, Whitehurst, McColl, Reynolds and Symons. The test was taken by Messrs. Fred Lester and Gavin Sampson qualified examiners of the B.S.L.A.

At Crackington Haven the same day eight members of the Crackington Surf Life Saving Club, formed 18-months ago, were taking part in B.S.L.A. examinations. Three of them—Roger Teague, Roy Tilley (vice-chairman) and Leonard B. Ward (captain and chairman)—gained their bronze medallions, and the other five, all young members, passed for their qualifying certificates. They were Stuart W. Dymond, Graham Sandercock, Denis J. Tape, Brian Teague and Paul A. Tilley. Messrs. Peter Boeck and David Docking (St. Agnes), were the examiners. These are the first examination results for this young, progressive club which is under the presidency of Wing Com. A. G. Parnall and has as its secretary Mr. H. W. Perkins.

him in. After resuscitation an ambulance was called and the patient was treated at Stratton Hospital, where all turned out well. It was a brave act on behalf of the swimmer, but my daughter just did what anyone else would have done. She was pleased to have played a part, even if a small one just to prove females could be useful! After that females were still strictly banned but she was quietly chuffed when they gave her a Surf Life Saving Club jumper. As they say, "got the tee shirt!" It was man-size, a bit sloppy back then but now, 50 years later, it fits perfectly! Nowadays the council employ lifeguards around the coast and they use another hut where I often see females!

Being on the coast there was always something happening. Folks often got caught out and cut off by the tide, Black Rock being a common spot. There is a completely secluded pool out there just right for a skinny-dip! It was one of my favourites, but you needed to keep an eye on the tide and be vigilant. Black Rock is only covered on the very highest tides so it's usually safe enough to sit it out. Roy's been out there at night to rescue people, using headlight beams, as they can get in a bit of a state as the water level rises. The scariest thing is when folks insist on climbing the cliffs. It happened quite frequently and of course it was really dangerous. Living here you develop a deep respect for the coast, natural surroundings and the force of nature. It's something you need to instil in each generation.

Courtesy © Streamline Photography & Design

Tremoutha Haven

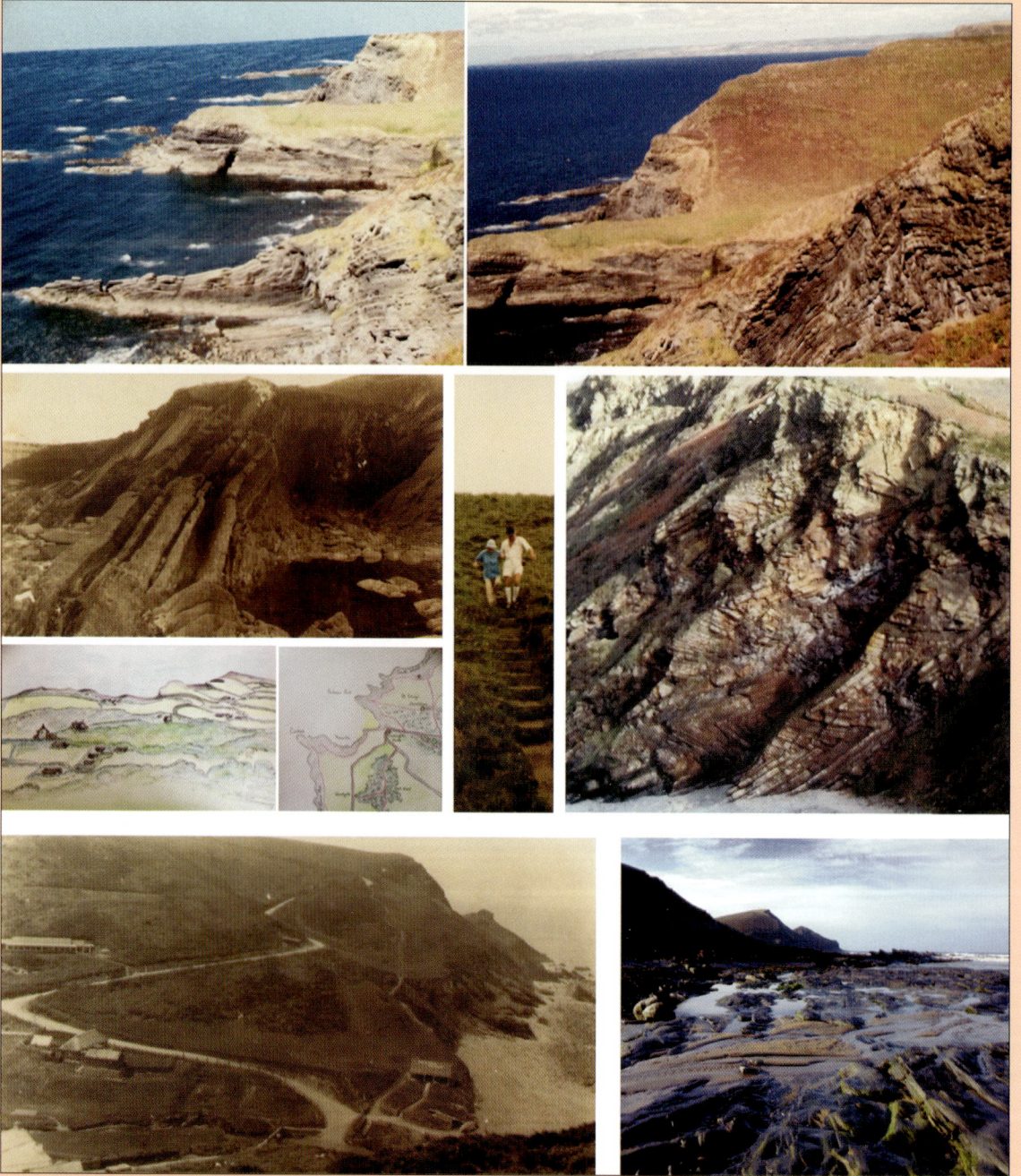

The coastal path
Views from Penkenna towards Bude.
Old pictures of the Big and Little Caves at Crackington and Millook

Chalets, Shacks and Sheds

The chalets of Crackington nestle into the landscape, the steep-sided valleys provide shelter from the coastal elements. Each generation has developed a deep affection for these quirky rustic homes, which were hidden away in secluded corners of this haven. In many instances the chalets were so secluded that only local families knew of their existence. Hence there has been much confusion over the use of the various wooden chalets and buildings. Some buildings that had been used for agriculture ended up being converted into residential dwellings, whereas other chalets that had been lived in were deemed unfit for habitation. They are disliked by some people, resulting in a struggle for those who want to renovate or replace them. Most have now been developed into conventional buildings, but there are still some chalets to be found. These homes exude nostalgia and charm reminiscent of earlier years; they predate many of the other buildings in the haven and each one has its own story.

There were originally six chalets in the Manor valley. The two nearest the orchards were Fitzhaven and Blaze, now developed and renamed Coombe Cottages. These were wooden with brick chimneys and fireplaces, they were popular with visitors and during the war they were occupied by evacuee families from London and Plymouth. There was a stone-built linhay near Blaze which housed animals, straw and feed. This building was also developed into a dwelling. In the valley, in front of Blaze, over the hedge from Grey Roofs' garden there is a meadow which we called The Platt. It is bordered by a stream with access across the flat bridge. We used to harvest hay there and carry it across the bridge to the meadow where we built the haystacks, near the cowshed. Tremar was built in the Platt by some close friends of my parents. Mrs Cox was a regular visitor at the Manor. In time they began to camp in the field beside the stream and eventually requested to rent some land to build a chalet for their holidays. It used to be common practice to permit people to place a transportable building for holidays. They paid for ground rent and, if no longer wanted, they had the option to remove it. There were three chalets in the Platt including Tremar. One was removed by its owner to a site elsewhere and another was swept away in the floods of the early 1900s. This was the first chalet to be lost to floods.

These were rustic chalets in an idyllic location, the stream trickled peacefully beside the garden and the sea was just a few minutes walk away. Fresh provisions were obtained from the Manor, while drinking water had to be carried. At that time there was no electric in the haven so paraffin lamps lit most homes and fires provided warmth and heat. The chalets had a veranda and some garden. Fitzhaven and Blaze were rented as holiday accommodation to visitors at the Manor. As for Tremar, the chalet remained in the same family for decades and then passed to the next generation of sisters, Ruth and Sheila. They bought the Platt, the field where Tremar stood, which included the flat bridge over the stream that my father had built with the chassis of the old Studebaker. Sheila was the single sister who had worked as a nursery teacher. She was wonderful with children and would take them on long hikes over the cliffs, picnics on the beach and held tea parties in the chalet garden. In return the children were happy to collect her water and provisions. When Sheila retired she sold her house and came to live at Tremar, which by then had a bathroom, telephone and other amenities. The third generation were now visiting their aunt at Tremar and both Ruth and Sheila were getting along in years. Sheila became physically ill and needed an operation and it was a mixed blessing that she was not there when the floods deluged the Platt in 2004. Unbeknown to her Tremar was swept away when the floods engulfed the valley, the chalet filled with water and collapsed under the pressure. It was a tragedy on all accounts because not only did Sheila lose her home, but also she never recovered from her operation. Ruth was caring for her family and her daughter was terminally ill, so when we phoned her to tell her about the floods we tried to break the news gradually by suggesting she watch the national news. She was devastated! Not only had she lost Tremar but she was to lose her sister and her daughter all at the same time! By the time Ruth came to visit with her son, any remains of Tremar, Ruth's caravan and the flat bridge had gone. A shred of curtain material was caught in a tree above them. If her caravan had not been removed she could have replaced it, but she found it all too much to bear. Tremar and Camryn suffered more than any other properties, the only ones to be completely demolished in the floods, but neither was eligible for flood relief or help. Looking into the valley now the remains of a fence and some hydrangea bushes survive, they flower in August each year, a memorial to our friends Sheila, Ruth and their chalet Tremar. Further up the valley on the south side of the river another chalet, Camryn, had suffered the same destruction. It was a similar story because the owner was elderly and never knew the outcome. Happily the younger family were able to escape the floods and, after much effort, Camryn was rebuilt on flood proof foundations. It is now a substantial log cabin and was featured in the filming of *Doc Martin* as the honeymoon lodge.

Hidden beyond Camryn is The Nook, a charming corrugated shack. It can be seen only from the orchards and has been there

Some chalets were purpose built for holidays while others like the first village hall, were

converted from old railway stock. Redundant carriages, wagons and huts were transported to the haven and converted into humble dwellings. These quirky, rustic

chalets exude the charm of a bygone era, although many have now been replaced or developed. Many chalets were occupied by evacuees during the war.

The beach cafés, surf club and tennis court hut all had humble beginnings.

as long as I can remember. In the next field, a private track leads to the Woodlands chalets that arrived some time after the First World War. Over the years they have had various owners, including friends of my sister Lottie. Throughout the parish there were a variety of chalets, some purpose built, while others were sectional or converted from wooden railway stock. I was younger when they were first situated here, but over the years I frequently drove visitors to and from the station. Whilst carrying paraffin and water they collected mail and provisions from the post office and could collect a meal from the Manor kitchen. In those days these chalets appealed to older people who were in a position to afford the services and ground rent and appreciate the peace and tranquillity of the area, away from civilisation. Today all the dwellings have been improved or replaced and have their own freehold and private access. There are three chalets in Lovers Lane, two purpose built and another that had been given a corner site with a humble beginning. In time the latter fell into the hands of twin sisters who desired to have a chalet each and so they had it cut in half! Both were turned around with one facing the east called Sunlight and the other west called Twilight. A communal kitchen was erected in the middle and both were happy. Later the chalets were burnt down and replaced by an old mobile home, which was in turn replaced later by a more sympathetic log cabin.

When Miss Palmer lived at Little Pen she had a wooden shed in the garden above the cottage, which she used as her library. Today it is a holiday chalet called Pencliff. Miss Palmer was a retired nurse who was always on hand to offer advice and attend to minor injuries. She had a stubborn donkey that refused to cross bridges and, more often than not, was seen being enticed by a carrot or two! Miss Palmer developed dementia and the roles reversed as my mother and sisters attended to her needs and provided her with meals. There were chalets at Ludon, Vera's mother lived in one of them before they were converted into stone residential dwellings. There were huts at the north side of the beachhead, and a surf shed on the south. In the old Manor asparagus garden there was a shed by the river. Coombe Barton had a chalet in the garden which is now converted into a stone-built dwelling and, of course, there were wooden beach shops and kiosks either end of the bridge. Love them or hate them, most wooden buildings have stood the test of time and will be found in many coastal areas around Cornwall. Many have lasted longer than their owners! They are unique and sit comfortably within the landscape and, in many cases, you don't even know they are there.

Tremar before and after the flood

Tremar, Blaze and the filming of *Doc Martin* at the honeymoon lodge, Camryn

Floods, Storms and Tempest

It was a calm sunny morning in Crackington on the 16th August 2004. Later that day emergency services were scrambled as Boscastle, Crackington Haven and Canworthy Water were deluged with floods. It was declared a National Disaster as torrents of water swelled through valleys ripping out everything in its path. At Boscastle people were being winched from rooftops by helicopter crews as buildings were destroyed and cars washed out to sea. In Crackington huge trees bobbed about like corks as they were tossed along in the swell. The water forced its way down through the haven and buildings were submerged in deep muddy water. It was a good thing it happened in daylight and no one was killed, but it left a lot of people in total shock and disbelief. In August the camping field was full of campers, the river burst its banks from the Ludon Valley creating havoc. Bill had been watching events unfold from his home on top of the hill and leapt into his Land Rover, but there was nothing anyone could do. It reminded me of years ago when one of Bill's sows was swept away in a flood. It hurtled down the river, under the bridge and out to sea. Bill managed to retrieve it and returned the sow to Ludon Farm where, in appreciation, it proceeded to give birth to a litter of piglets! This time further up the Congdons and Coombe Valley the river left its bed and rose to over 20ft high in places. Rocks, stones and debris washed onto the fields and a footbridge in the old Manor orchard ended up precariously lodged in a treetop. The chalets near the water's edge didn't stand a chance and a family had to clamber over a hedge to safety. You could only watch in disbelief as the water rose dramatically in a raging torrent. There was much confusion as hedges, fences and boundaries disappeared – and there was devastation at the beachhead. Prince Charles kindly came to visit the area some time after and I had the pleasure of meeting him. I met his mother and aunt some years ago at Kelly Bray when the Royal Cornwall Show was held there. There was no showground at Wadebridge in those days and the Princesses Elizabeth and Margaret were young teenagers. I remember it was held in a field and it poured with rain all day, so everyone got stuck. They must have had a pretty good impression of Cornwall!

There have always been floods in Crackington; it is inevitable in certain conditions. Over the years riverbanks have been built up, but on high tides the sea can reach the bridge and beyond. Heavy rainfall swells the rivers and water backs up in a narrow valley. We used to watch the waves wash over the beachhead and flow over the bridge, waves would travel up the river as far as the footbridge. Over the century I have seen the weather patterns change. The winters were always long and cold with freezing conditions; we used to get snow and sometimes we would be cut off for days and, in some instances, even weeks. I have seen the sand freeze. You could skate on the ice and admire long icicles hanging from Penkenna. We were always prepared for bad weather and kept provisions stocked throughout the winter. I remember a hailstorm that smashed glass and dented car roofs because the hailstones were as big as golf balls. These days winters are warmer and milder. There have always been strong storms and coastal gales, but now they are extreme and often hurricane force, which is far more damaging. When the wind whips up the waves of the sea it can result in a foam storm. With Crackington being a narrow haven the effect is enhanced. Foam looks like snow when it covers the ground and the sea turns into a colossal meringue! I was on the bridge for Storm Imogen when winds were up to 90mph and waves over 40ft hit the coast in 2016.

The Great Blizzard of Cornwall
In 1891 there was a snowstorm that brought Cornwall to a standstill, as violent gales blew down trees and snow drifted up to 15ft. This happened during the life of my parents; my grandparents were farming in Crackington at the time. Not only was Cornwall brought to a standstill, but also every household and farm in St Gennys was cut-off and isolated. It had already been a hard freezing winter and then the blizzard arrived in March, when no doubt everyone was turning their attention to spring. You may imagine that people could light the fire and stay indoors, but that was not possible as the sub-zero temperatures plummeted for at least a week. There was no electricity, running water or central heating. Logs would be kept outside and, with snow piled 15ft high against your door and windows, you would be trapped inside in the dark! We can imagine the severe gale-force winds from the east, but it is difficult to envisage how they coped or even survived under such harsh conditions. My father was 11-years-old at the time and for certain he would have been out with the shovel digging his way through the snow. Water would have frozen solid and outside the animals, horses and other livestock would perish under snowdrifts. In fact an estimated 6,000 animals and about 200 people lost their lives in that blizzard.

No one could communicate under those conditions. With no phones, televisions or radios people would have no idea what was happening in the world outside or how long the freezing conditions would last. These days if you experience snowfall everyone expects it to be cleared and there are weather forecasts and news reports to

Floods in August 1950 at Crackington and an old picture of Boscastle

Floods which deluged Boscastle and Crackington in 2004 and the visit of Prince Charles

Storm Imogen 2016 and floods of 2004

Storm on the bridge February 2016

keep you up-to-date. The blizzard occurred at the same time as the railway was being built between Launceston and Otterham, so it's little wonder that they found it hard. Trains vanished under snowdrifts and dozens of ships were caught in the gales and sank at sea.

After the great thaw no doubt the ground would have been saturated and crops ruined. I can't imagine the sheep or their lambs would have survived, and there were no shops or supermarkets to replenish the larder. It must have been tough to get through these storms and the freezing conditions. Now, like everything else, the pendulum has swung to the other extreme and they tell us 2015 was the warmest year on record!

Linda on the frozen Manor millpond in the 1950s

Cut off by snow and ice 1963

The Children of St Gennys

It has never been easy keeping track of everyone, but my father did. He would start at one end of the parish and work his way around naming each family member until he reached the other side. As for the family history in St Gennys, that will fill another book! We had dozens of cousins, aunts and uncles throughout the parish, we were a very close-knit community. Maybe that's frowned upon these days, but having lived through both past and present I can make a comparison. It may seem old-fashioned now but we were happy and content with life, even if we met with challenges. Working hard gave us satisfaction and a feeling of accomplishment and we all worked and played together.

We made our own entertainment, even producing and performing our own concerts. During evenings we sat around the large open fires and played cards. The men usually played billiards in the drawing room, while the women did some sewing or knitting. Even the budgie was sociable! My mother would release it from its cage and it would fly freely around the room before landing on a head or shoulder to have a chat. Before the village institute was built in the 1950s we held social evenings, dances and whist drives at the Manor. There were tennis courts in Crackington, finely cut by a horse-drawn mower; the horse wore leather boots to avoid leaving hoof marks. With so much work to do our leisure time was precious and often we would squeeze in an early dip before breakfast. There was never a dull moment. Yet, with no one around in those days, it was so peaceful and tranquil. The waves would gently lap onto the shore as the sun rose over the valley. The men enjoyed band music and St Gennys has always had a good silver band. When they started out my father said they could only play one tune! At their first venue, The Little Brown Jug, they played it over and over again. On

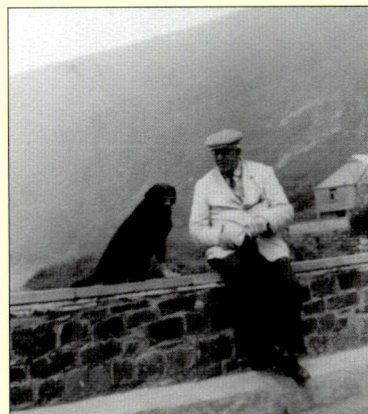

My father lived to a good age

summer evenings our cousins and friends congregated for some fun and there was always plenty of it. Our lives were action packed, full of fun and laughter and we all had a very happy and healthy childhood.

My father died in the 1960s. It was a traumatic time for the entire family and would signal some big changes, not only for the family but also for the whole of Crackington. He had lived through two world wars and had put his heart and soul into building a future for his family. The Second World War took its toll, there was so much pressure from every angle and it seemed all his plans were cast aside. It was compulsory to take in evacuees and the Manor was full to overflowing. The future was uncertain but he had recovered from all that and lived to a good age. It didn't seem possible that someone so strong could die! He passed away in his room overlooking the sea and we had never prepared for such an event. When the time came everyone turned out and formed a line either side of the garden path. They sang hymns as he was carried out, that was the Cornish tradition. He was laid to rest at the cemetery on top of the hill on the south side along with my grandparents. My mother wept, she was left tired and weary with grief. For the first time in her life she was unable to cope and went to live with my sister.

As for Crackington Manor, the family were all married and had children and businesses of their own. Everyone wanted the Manor to stay in the family as that's what my father intended. It was offered to each one in turn, but we all knew the amount of work involved and there were

five of us to share. We all lived to regret our decisions as, in time, everything became so much easier, but you can't go back. I carried on with Manor Cottage, which I had bought from my father. Later I had my hands full when Martha became terminally ill, especially with the garage, beach shop and coaching business now in full swing. My wife died, an unexpected shock as she wasn't very old. I gradually handed over the businesses to the next generation and eventually retired. I remarried again later in life and my new wife enjoyed travel and holidays. We also walked the coast paths but she too suffered ill health. I have been alone for several years now but have good friends and family and still enjoy a good social life. My latest mode of transport is a 4mph mobility scooter, which is a far cry from the old Studebaker and Crossley I started out with! When I look back, which I often do, I realise just how much my parents did for us. We couldn't have been born into a better family or a more beautiful part of the world.

End of an era

Lottie Grace Tilley

My eldest sister was delighted to receive her card from the queen when she reached 100! Lottie and I were both born at Hill Farm at the top of Crackington. We don't remember much about it because we moved to the Manor when we were very young. She has been the typical older sibling, always there to watch out for me and rescue me from trouble. We had a lot in common; to start with we were the only siblings to use our first names. We walked miles together and attended school and Sunday school side-by-side. The footpath to Sunday school was from Ludon Gate up over the field where Paramatta (Spindrift) and Gunedah were eventually built. This was one of the finest paths with fabulous views from the top of Mill Ball over the whole haven and out to sea. On the way down, in spite of warnings from Lottie, it was impossible to avoid the desire to slide from top to bottom on my backside! By the time I reached Ludon Gate I had ripped my trousers, resulting in the inevitable scalding from mother. Lottie was a keen churchgoer, whereas I would escape it if I could. It was a recognised thing in those days to attend church on Sundays, sometimes twice a day. That wasn't too bad in the winter, but when the sun shone I would do everything in my power to avoid it! All the usual excuses of tummy ache, headache or even hiding away until it was too late. Looking back I think it was good to learn some moral principles, but you have to work things out as you go through life. I have never influenced my own family in matters of religion or politics. Lottie and I both left school at fourteen and worked at home with our parents and on the farm. She was very keen on all countryside matters and knew all the wildlife, birds, flowers and plants. She worked hard on the farm, post office and in the Manor and even had her own sideline where she sold local pottery and some leather goods in the post office store. Everyone recognised Lottie with her long hair usually plaited up into buns on either ear, probably fashionable during the 1920s but she kept them for life! She always looked well dressed, never wore trousers but then women didn't years ago. She has never had her hair cut or worn lipstick and I've never heard her swear, other than the occasional "darn or blast it!" She was just a good honest, hard-working country girl. During the war it was Lottie that cared for the Dutch crew from the stranded cargo ship. She was popular with everyone she met and made a perfect host to welcome visitors to the Manor.

Lottie married Gordon Heal, another local farmer. He joined the family in the Manor and together they took care of the farm. Like most of us Gordon played in the St Gennys band, it was a family tradition. They had a daughter, Linda, and it wasn't until later in the 1960s that they moved to Bude where they ran a guesthouse of their own. Lottie has a strong constitution and you never hear her complain. She lost her daughter to cancer many years ago, then her husband Gordon died. She managed amazingly well on her own, in spite of losing her sight. Lottie was already blind in one eye due to an accident on the farm years before, and

Lottie Grace Tilley and Gordon Heal

now the other eye had lost vision. A remarkable woman, she became housebound but there was nothing to deter her from keeping busy. She grew her own vegetables, the greenhouse was full to bursting with tomatoes and cucumbers all grown from seed. Everyone that called to see Lottie would have the job of threading needles with various coloured cottons and preparing patches for her quilts. A patchwork quilt was made up from snippets of material, bits and pieces of clothing worn by our mother, daughters and Lottie's own frocks and aprons from years gone by. Some snippets were well over 150 years old, but nothing was wasted and every patch was patiently stitched, mostly by touch, into some wonderful quilts of life. If you are a dedicated follower of fashion you may be able to match the pattern design to the era. In the kitchen Lottie carried on cooking, her freezer was full. Everything in the house remained in exactly the same position for years, as if anything was to be moved or turned around she would be lost. If you took her a bunch of flowers the chances were, the next time you called, she would produce the plant from the cuttings! She had green fingers and could get anything to grow. After a bad fall she became immobile and moved to a residential home, where she is still bright and cheerful. She follows sport and quiz programmes, is always interested in others and asks about Crackington and the Manor. If you climb Penkenna Cliff you may be glad to have a rest at the top where Lottie donated the bench to the National Trust to remember the family. For some reason, however, she was not permitted an inscription back then. Everyone can stop for a while and take a bird's-eye view of the haven and the coast beyond, the same view as Lottie and her family loved so much.

Loveday Eileen Tilley
My next sister was named after our aunt Loveday, a lovely Cornish name but often called Eileen. Eileen was nine or ten years younger than myself and also helped out at home until she married in the early 1950s. Cleaning brass was just one of her responsibilities and there was a lot of it: fenders, doorknobs and stair rods to mention a few. There was no stainless steel in those days so all cutlery, utensils and tableware needed a polish. The many fireplaces from the large cooking range, huge open fireplaces down to the little bedroom fires all needed cleaning and polishing black. The oak panelling in the drawing room was polished with beeswax, whilst floors were scrubbed and carpets beaten. In the big downstairs kitchen a large wood-fired boiler was used for washing (no washing machines then), and all starched and ironed with flat irons heated on the fire. Everyone helped on the farm and took their turn at milking.

Eileen married Percy Cowling in the early 1950s. His father, Jethro Cowling, came from Jacobstow and Canworthy Water. Percy cycled to Crackington to meet up with my sister. I suppose years ago there were a lot of young men cycling or galloping from nearby parishes to find themselves a wife. The couple had a difficult time when Percy became critically

ST. GENNYS.

WEDDING: COWLING—TILLEY.

Bride's Niece Christened After Ceremony.

Brockhill Methodist Church was the scene of a pretty wedding on Friday week, having been decorated with summer flowers by members and friends. The contracting parties were Mr. Percy Cowling (elder son of Mr. and Mrs. J. Cowling, of Tuckingmill, Canworthy Water) and Miss Loveday Eileen Tilley (youngest daughter of Mr. and Mrs. W. T. Tilley, of Manor House, Crackington Haven). Escorted by her brother (Mr. Alfred Tilley), the bride wore a full-length gown of white figured satin, with a yoke of net, embroidered with sequins and crystal beads; a full-length embroidered veil, and coronet of orange blossom (lent by a friend), and white shoes. She carried a bouquet of white iris and red roses and trailing fern. The chief bridesmaid was Miss Christine Cowling (sister of groom), who wore a full-length dress of lilac art. silk taffeta, white shoes, and head-dress of white flowers, and carried a bouquet of mixed anemones. The "Tiny Tot" bridesmaid was little Julia Tilley (niece of bride), who wore an ankle-length dress of peach flowered organdie, white shoes, and head-dress of white flowers and silver leaves, and carried a posy of mixed anemones. The best man was Mr. Fernley Collier (brother-in-law of groom). Rev. N. Gilson, M.A., officiated, and the organist was Miss Edith Ward (cousin of bride). Customary gifts were exchanged, and the bridegroom's gift to the elder bridesmaid was a pendant and chain, and to the younger bridesmaid, a gold bracelet. The reception was held at the home of the bride, after which the happy couple left for their honeymoon in London, the bride travelling in a dress of check silk taffeta, with fawn and brown coat, and accessories to match. The bride's bouquet was later placed on her cousin's grave at Brockhill. The future home will be at Canworthy Water.

After the reception, Mr. Gilson christened the bride's niece, Linda Margaret. She is the infant daughter of Mr. and Mrs. G. Hea[?], of Crackington Haven. Mrs. P. Ward and Mrs. A. Tilley (aunts) were the God-parents.

Loveday Eileen and family

ill; he managed to pull through in spite of no penicillin. In those days if you had a bad infection there were no antibiotics and, in his case, the only option was amputation. A prosthetic leg was wooden and cumbersome, but if ever a man showed determination it was Percy. My parents worried and, from my father's point of view, if you couldn't work then you didn't get paid. Percy was a farmer and there was no chance of returning to that occupation. There were no disability benefits back then and it must have been very hard getting around, let alone earning a living. I had the privilege of giving my sister Eileen away on her wedding day. My daughter was a toddler bridesmaid and Percy's sister the chief. The reception was held at the Manor and photographs taken at the ceremony illustrate how times had changed since the war. A white wedding! Father soon came around to the idea and it was a marriage that ended happily ever after. He need not have worried; Percy and Eileen were a very determined couple and worked like Trojans. They had a plot of land large enough to build themselves a bungalow and keep some animals. They did all the building work themselves and set up a taxi business and a newspaper round. There was nothing they couldn't accomplish with just three legs, but not everything worked to plan. When they set up a mushroom farm the compost was kept in the dark for some while, but nothing appeared to grow. Giving up, Eileen threw all the compost out onto the garden and, would you believe it, one morning the garden was white with

Esther Monica with siblings (top picture). Eldest son Trevor (middle left). Young Biscombe children with cousins. Wedding reception of Carolyn Biscombe, held at Crackington Manor

button mushrooms! The couple had three children, two of which married and emigrated to Australia. Victor is a carpenter and Raymond an international artist who has been commissioned for some amazing sculptures. Raymond and wife Lisa have travelled the world but have returned to the Cornish coast more recently. In later life Eileen had a bilateral hip replacement. I had the same operation myself a few years ago, unusual to have two in the same family! Eventually Percy and Eileen joined their family in Australia, they shipped their possessions, including the wooden leg, and soon settled into a new way of life down under. By the time they'd emigrated they only had one good leg between them!

Esther Monica Tilley

The youngest sister who preferred to be called Monica worked as the post office assistant; she was responsible for sorting the mail and serving customers. In those days she sent and received telegrams and, with no bank nearby, locals depended on the post office savings counter. Monica also married a farmer, John Biscombe. They too lived and helped out in the Manor until they were able to take over the smallholding at Sweets, which is at the top of Crackington. Here they raised six children, four boys and two girls. John had a broad Cornish dialect and I didn't always catch what he said, but he had a ready smile and had good command of the family. Sweets was a small traditional Cornish cottage with sufficient ground and a good orchard. The children spent a lot of time with their mother at the Manor; the cousins all got along very well and had complete freedom of the haven. You didn't worry about your children in those days; they looked after each other and were free to play outdoors in the fresh air. There was very little traffic, you could hear a car coming from a mile away and more often than not you knew who would be arriving. Children didn't have many toys back then, they made their own fun and there were always plenty of chores to do. The girls take after their mother, the youngest daughter Angela and her husband now also run a post office, no doubt it's very different in comparison to her mother's job all those years ago. The boys took up farming, carpentry and maintenance work. Trevor was

William Roy on his wedding day. Earlier days on his motorbike and at the Manor. Daughter Sandra as a bridesmaid in 1972

Alfred and Lottie

Lottie and Gordon's wedding at the Manor

the eldest son, he was born in the Manor and has lived locally ever since. He has meticulously maintained many of the homes in the area including Tremar and Camryn, which were both lost to the floods. Chris and Peter worked locally while Roger took off to Scotland – from one end of the kingdom to the other! When Carolyn married she arranged the reception to be held at Crackington Manor in the same tradition as her parents. Monica was my youngest sister and died some years ago. It is a strange feeling when you outlive the younger ones.

William Roy Tilley
William Roy was the youngest of us all and the last to marry. He took after my father in many respects and could turn his hand to anything. We had both been responsible for the post round. My father had established the post office in the haven and we delivered the mail by foot. We covered several miles around the parish, which was quite a marathon. The postal route became the recognised footpaths in the parish and can be enjoyed at a more leisurely pace today! In those days many people sent telegrams, which needed to be delivered at once and there could be several in a day. Roy was artistic, creative and had a great sense of humour. We shared the same passion for engineering and he built his own vehicles, all tried and tested on hill trials. After doing national service Roy was sent to Egypt where he became a military policeman but, like me, he was keen to return home. He was just a young boy when I volunteered for the army so I missed seeing him grow up, but I know he would have been a great asset to my father during those years. We both became professional drivers and between us we covered every nook and cranny of Cornwall. Roy was a family man with a son, daughter and grandchildren living locally. He married Pam and designed and built a family house before moving to Higher Crackington. He always appeared fit and healthy and I certainly never expected to live longer than my youngest brother.

St Gennys Band

1907–1909 From back row: Rocky Smeeth, Ewart Gliddon, John Heal, Mark Wickett, Claude Sandercock, Harold Patten, John Goodman, Edward Heal, ?, Charles Heal, William Tilley (right).
Second row left: Ern Gliddon, Percy Heal, Ambrose Sandercock, Tom Ward, Heywood Cowling, Band Master Cook, Charles Cowling, Cecil Heal, Ern Brookham, Bryant Heal.
Front row: Edgar Ward, Claude Spry, Alfred Ward, Tom Sandercock.

1940s winning the cup

Above: Lottie, Alfred and Eileen
Eva, Evelyn and Julia
Left: Reunion at Eagle House.
Farewell to Ian, Jessica and family as
they leave for Melbourne, Australia.

Family reunions with our Australian relations

1950s Fun on the bridge.   St Gennys girls at the Country Dance Festival.
1940s Paul by a Studebaker wheel.   Young Clive Tilley and later on the bike with Ivor Ward.
1950s The Tilley family at the Carnival - The Water Babes and Polly put the kettle on.
1950s School days - Clive and Julia at St Gennys school.

Frank and Mary Ward celebrating.
Rex and Cheryl.
Little Melrose built by Fred and Jane Edwards.
Bottom: The Smeeth and Pearce family and Bide A Wee, the Linhay and chalet in the Platt below.
A view of the haven in the 1920s

The family of Frank and Ruth Tape

Frank was best known as a master stonemason, many of the stone walls and buildings around St Gennys featured his handy work. His heritage skills were put to good effect at Tintagel castle where there was a lot of restoration work and we were grateful for his plastering skills when we extended the Manor. He was a keen member of the St Gennys band playing the euphonium. Frank married my sister-in-law and they built their home at Havenward before the days of electricity and running water. They raised four children: Rodney who joined the Royal Airforce; Dennis who was a keen surf club member and later served in the army where he was awarded the MBE; Jocelyn married and moved to Bedford and Philip, who was a keen bandsman, remained in Cornwall. Ruth used to attend all the local events in St Gennys and was the reporter of local news for many years.

Country holidays in Crackington 1940s & 1950s enjoying time with our family

Carson Foster

Winifred from Canada

Jill Pettifer – a regular guest

Janet and Christine Clements were frequent visitors from London

The Richardsons (above) – memorable times with our family at Tremar in the early 1950s

The Pearce girls (left and below) with Julia, Ruth Punton, David and June Davis

Ancestry, Trees and Timeline

Ancestry, Trees and Timeline

Timeline

1540 Barton of Treworgie on lease to the Mill family.
1586 First potatoes arrive at Plymouth.
1593 Benet Mill – the Mill family. Grave at St Gennys.
1601 Poor Act cottages at Pencuke and Churchtown.
1622 Harvest failure.
1641 Bray family (Joan m Thomas Mill).
1693 Stephen Bray left twenty shillings to the poor of St Gennys.
1723 Workhouses established.
1737 Thomas Jago.
1739 Survey of Manor tenants.
1744 Charles Wesley visits St Gennys.
1748 John and Ann Mill.
1768 Mary Mill and John Tilley.
1775 William Bray is the parish clerk.
1808 Thomas Tilley and Maria Isbel Jago.
1815 Edward and Mary Mill hold Bible meetings at home.
1818 William Sandercock.
1834 Workhouse for Stratton, Thomas Jago and others protested.
1836 Plans for harbour, station and town at Crackington.
1838 Mary Mill buried at St Gennys Church, first nonconformist funeral.
1839 Photography invented.

1842 Thomas Jago Tilley.
1842 Brockhill Methodist.
1844 Grace Sandercock.
1857 John HP and Ann Ward (both born on the same day).
1862 Tremayna Methodist.
1891 Great Blizzard of Cornwall.
1893 Otterham Station opened.
1895 School closed for three weeks, whooping cough and flu.
1914 World War 1.
1916 Battle of the Somme, France.
1918 Spanish flu. Pandemic.
1920 Crackington Manor Estate divided up.
1928 Penicillin discovered – not used until later in 1940s.
1930 Post office established in Crackington.
1935 Beach purchased from Duchy.
1939 World War 2.
1945 Town and Country Planning introduced.
1947 Cut off by snow for three weeks.
1950s Electricity, water and telephones arrive.
1950s Road bridge constructed and roads improved.
1954 Rationing ends.
1955 Crackington Institute built to replace the Men's Club.
1960s Otterham Station closed, last train.
1970s New housing estate built at Brockhill. First street lights and pavements.

Ancestry

Those interested in family history don't have to look far. Most of our ancestors were laid to rest in St Gennys churchyard, over the other side of Penkenna Cliff on the north side. As you enter the gate my great grandparents are to be found either side of the path. Many of the inscriptions are worn by age, but a closer look will reveal each further generation. Mary Mill became the first nonconformist to be buried in St Gennys churchyard, as neither Tremayna nor Brockhill chapels had been built. Once Brockhill became established then the cemetery on the south side became the resting place of my grandparents and our extended family.

The first mention of my grandmother's family we found recorded in the late 1600s, around the time that crown glass was made, Fort William was built in the Scottish Highlands and before Abraham Darby pioneered iron smelting!

At that time most people lived in the countryside and earned a living by farming. Seed was sown by hand and broadcast over the soil until about 1701. The first potatoes had arrived in Plymouth in 1586. Both grain and potatoes coexisted and were nutritious. Potatoes were able to produce more calories per acre and they didn't require grinding, but grain was easier to store. Men wore breeches and frock coats and

Family life over the past centuries

women wore hooped petticoats under their dresses. Both men and women wore wigs and they transported all their goods by packhorse. Our ancestors had a hard time eking out a living, they had to be frugal. Records indicate that Cornish farmers managed their farms well, but there was a harvest failure in St Gennys in 1622. There were provisions made for the poor and it was in the 1600s that cottages were built at Pencuke and Churchtown to help provide for them. There is evidence that everyone pulled together and helped one another out. When Stephen Bray died he left twenty shillings to the poor of St Gennys, which was a generous amount in those days. My ancestor Thomas Jago was seriously opposed to the building of a workhouse in Stratton, he wasn't the only one. In fact throughout Cornwall there were protests to the union workhouses. These institutions were cruel and little more than imprisonment to hard toil and slavery, with no chance of recovery or self-help. Over the centuries there were many Thomas Jagos and it's easy to get confused. My grandfather was Thomas Jago Tilley but, prior to him, there were many other Thomas Jagos as families often carried on with the same name. For example: Thomas Jago in 1648, then Thomas Jago from Plynt who married Elizabeth Hickes; Thomas Jago who first married Honour Potter in St Gennys and then Elizabeth Isbell. (Richard Isbell married Lydia Bligh); another Thomas Jago married Grace Rundle, he was born at Laneast and married in Jacobstow. My great grandmother was Maria Isbel Jago.

They were all born in Cornwall.

Research into the Tilley side of the family has proved more difficult and, judging by the letters received from overseas searching for information, we are not the only ones finding it hard. My ancestor and great-great-great grandfather was John Tilley and he married Mary Mill, a local couple. Research beyond this is still in progress. It would appear the Tilley family originated from Northern France and there were mentions of Tilleys in the Domesday Book. The surname has been found in Sussex, Bedfordshire and Somerset, but we have yet to discover how they ended up in Cornwall. It is of no surprise to learn that many of our ancestors emigrated in search of a better life and we know that many of the Tilley family were among those who left. The Mayflower story is interesting because, regardless of whether they are ancestors or not, it provides an accurate account of the hardships they endured sailing across the pond. It was the Mayflower Compact that made this group significant, because there had been others who had sailed to America before them. However, little is known about how they got on or what became of them. The group of Pilgrims that left Plymouth in 1620 were known as Separatists. They were persecuted at having left the mainstream church; they found it too powerful and did not approve of the traditions and elaborate ceremonies. I imagine they would have been a humble and modest crowd with great integrity and courage. On arrival they signed the Compact which, in time, set the stage for the Constitution of the United States of America. I wonder what they would think if they knew. Their voyage surely gives us an insight into the extremes people went to and what they endured in order to find a better life. I imagine the voyage was precarious especially as The Mayflower was an old freighter, tired and worn after years of carrying cargo. The departure was delayed and September was not a good month to set sail across the Atlantic. It took over nine weeks to reach America. Life on board was documented by Bradford and he described it as grim, just a matter of survival! People huddled together in groups while the seas pounded and freezing water cascaded over them. Passengers had little chance to sleep as there were howling gales and slamming sails. John Howland was tossed overboard but was hauled back. Two passengers died and Elizabeth Hopkins gave birth to a baby named Oceanus. When they arrived their supplies were dwindling, scurvy and pneumonia were rife and the group was reduced including, sadly, baby Oceanus. Among the group were John and Edward Tilley with some family. The brothers had signed the Compact and they were amongst the volunteers for an expedition. They encountered freezing and foul weather, their clothes stuck to them and they suffered frostbite and died the following year in 1621. John had taken his daughter Elizabeth with him to America and she later married John Howland, the man who had been tossed overboard. They went on to have children and there are

many descendants from them living in America today. When John and Edward sailed from England they left behind other family, but they have become known as the "Lost Tilleys". One son, Robert, was recorded as serving an apprenticeship as a tailor and a daughter, Rose, later married. This may explain why neither of them travelled to America. In 1623 another John Tilley arrived in America, but there is little relating to him and he may have been killed by Indians. In 1717 there was a will published relating to William Tilley of Boston, he was a rope-maker and left £20 to his brother John and £10 to his sister Elinor, both living in Topsham, Devonshire. William had settled in Boston and had bought a large tract of land on which he erected a rope walk. The street east of this is named Tilleys Lane and the wharf is called Tilleys Wharf. The search for the missing Tilleys continues.

As for my grandmother Grace, she was the youngest of a family of eleven children living at Pencuke, which is to the north of Crackington. The first of the Sandercock family was recorded in the late 1600s. My grandmother's grandmother was Grace Bray and she married Richard Sandercock. They had two daughters, one also named Grace who was a dressmaker and, at that time, they would have dressed in the long and elegant Jane Austen style. They had nine children, one of their sons Stephen was a tailor and the youngest son, William, was my great grandfather. It must have been a busy household what with running a farm and a kitchen table filled with material and sewing. The Royal Mail Coaching Service was established by this time, making travel and communication a bit easier. My grandmother Grace was the youngest child of William and Mary Sandercock and she married Thomas Jago Tilley in the Victorian era. It seems they tried to break from farming as Thomas joined the police force and the couple moved to Exeter where he served as PC Tilley Officer No 13. The 1871 census records them as living in Friernhay Street with their eldest son James aged one year. The penny-farthing was invented in 1871 and they may have seen a few flying around Exeter. Eventually the couple returned to live at Otterham where my grandfather was employed as a farm bailiff. My father was born at Otterham followed by Alfred, who was the youngest and was born at Flanders Farm in Crackington. It must have been a stark contrast moving from a farm in Crackington to Exeter. Serving in the police force in a city would not have been easy. There is mention of PC Tilley in the records when he hit the news for charging someone with hauling putrid matter through the town, the magistrates inflicting a penalty of two shillings and sixpence plus costs. Around the same time a man was charged for losing control of two horses and a wagon. Grace spent hours alone with her son and another new baby, Mary Elizabeth. I can imagine they must have missed the family at Crackington. The couple were all too familiar with the trials and tribulations associated with agriculture, but they were clearly happy to return home and take up farming again. After Flanders my grandfather became a tenant to the Crackington Manor estate and farmed at Hill. I remember my grandparents, Thomas and Grace, very well. My father and I converted Manor Cottage for their retirement, so they lived next door for many years. My grandfather used to help around the garden and on the farm while my other grandparents lived at the top of the hill. They were also frequent visitors to the Manor. It's hardly surprising that the family filled the parish. I struggle to keep account with nearly 40 cousins and most have married locally – it's quite a happy family! Harry Polatch was ex Royal Navy and he married our cousin Rose Sandercock and her sister, Dorothy Sandercock, married a Teague and so it went on.... Northcotts, Biscombes, Gliddons, Wards etc, etc. The Teagues are good builders and have built many of the homes in Crackington from the early days and up until recently. Someone once whispered in my ear, "Be careful what you say when you are talking about anyone around here, because they are all related". I smiled, but mother would have said, "If you can't say something to their face you shouldn't say it at all". Harry drove an Austin 7 and used to come down Mill Ball hill with his head poking through the sunshine roof. One day Harry was collecting aunt Loveday for a visit to the Manor when he had a slight collision at Otterham. Harry was a joker, always laughing his head off. "If we had all been killed then the whole parish would have been out in mourning!" he said. That just about summed it up!

Esther Kate Ward in the 1880s

Filleys
John Filley and Mary Mill
Thomas and Elizabeth
Thomas and Maria Isbell Jago
Thomas Jago Filley and Grace Sandercock
William Thomas Filley and Esther Kate Ward

Brays
William and ?
John Bray & Ann
Stephen Bray &?
William and Margaret Wickett
John and Lucie Marshall
Stephen and Katherine French
Stephen and Grace Bray
Grace Bray & Richard Sandercock
William Sandercock & Mary Goodman
Grace Sandercock & Thomas Jago Filley
William Thomas Filley

Hurdle. Hawkey. Vosper
Richard Vosper and Elizabeth Hawkey
John Hurdle and Jane Vosper
Katurah Hudle and James Jago
Maria Isbel Jago and Thomas Filley
Thomas Jago Filley and Grace Sandercock
William Thomas Filley and Esther Kate Ward

Rundles
Charles Rundle and Catherine Smeeth
William Rundle and Genny Marshall
Ann Rundle and John H.P. Ward
Esther Kate and William Thomas Filley

Jago
Thomas Jago and Grace
Richard Jago and Jane Sym
William Jago and Elizabeth Webber
Thomas Jago and Elizabeth Hicks
James Jago and Katurah Hurdle
Maria Isbel Jago and Thomas Filley
Thomas Jago Filley and Grace Sandercock
William Thomas Filley

Wards
Edward and Elizabeth
Edward and Grace Marshall
William and Margaret Crews
Edward and Loveday Robins
Edward and Mary Finny
William and Wilmot Jolliffe
William and Grace Pearce
John H.P. Ward and Ann Rundle
Esther Kate Ward

Sandercocks
Robert and Mary
Robert and Mary Dennis
Robert and Grace Robins
Richard and Grace Bray
William and Mary Goodman
Grace and Thomas Jago Filley
William Thomas Filley

Jago
William Jago and Elizabeth
Thomas And Elizabeth Hicks
James and Katurah Hurdle
Maria Isbell and Thomas Filley
Thomas Jago Filley and Grace Sandercock
William Thomas Filley

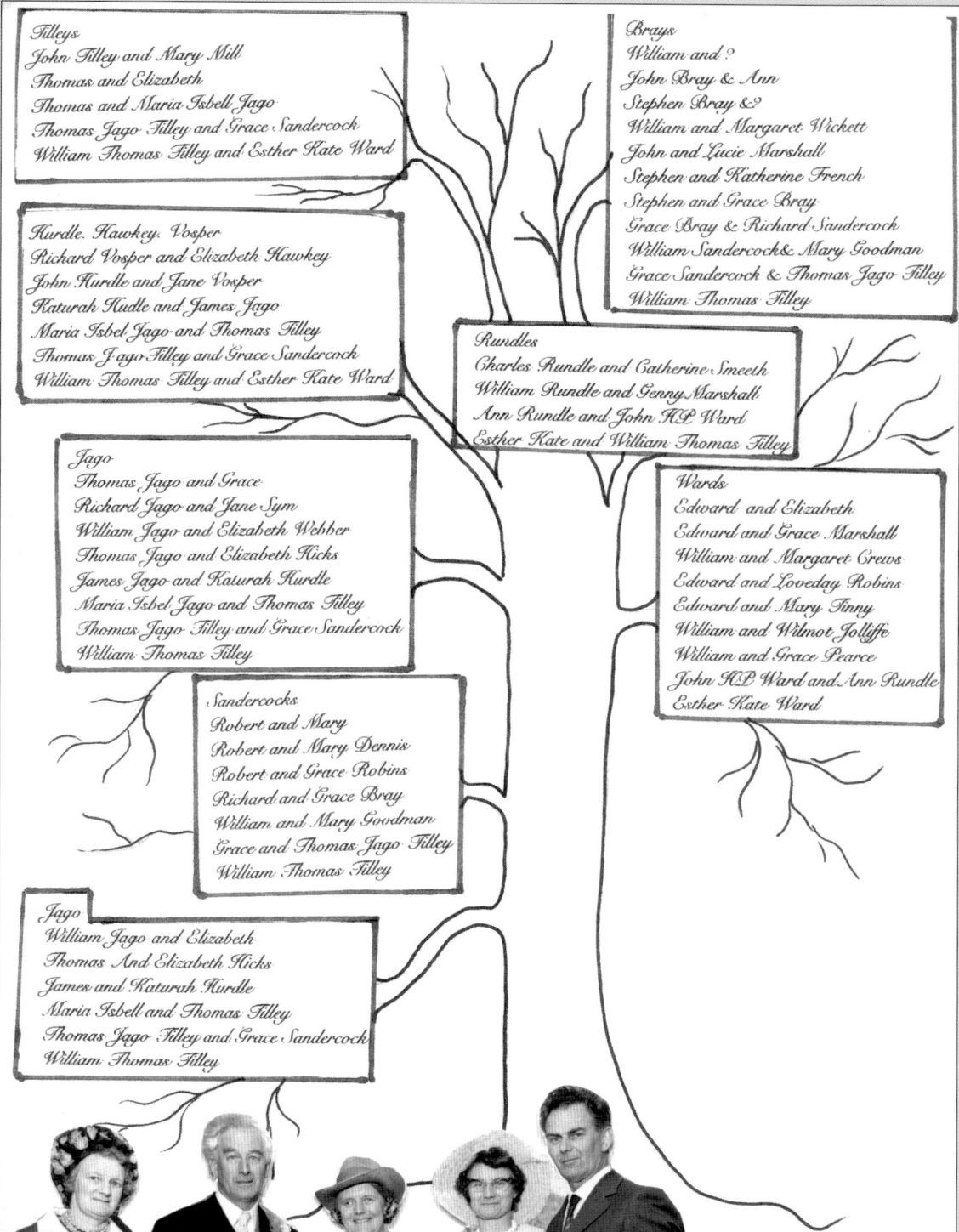

Local Direct Ancestry

Family resting in peace at Brockhill and St Gennys

Cheers!